קולות

KOLOT:

Celebrating the Plurality of Jewish Voices

Published by Valley Beit Midrash

Volume I   Fall 2014/5775

Valley Beit Midrash

I would like to welcome you to both Valley Beit Midrash and to our new publication *KOLOT: Celebrating the Plurality of Jewish Voices.*

Valley Beit Midrash (VBM) is a collaborative organization that brings new, exciting, and relevant programs to the Greater Phoenix Jewish community in a diverse, welcoming, engaging, and pluralistic setting. VBM also leads the Start Me Up! Fellowship to inspire and support transformative innovation throughout the community, as well as the newly introduced Jewish Leadership Corps, a cutting-edge new fellowship program that trains and supports emerging dynamic Jewish leaders in their twenties.

Throughout our seven years of classes, speakers, and panels, we knew we were sitting on a gold mine of ideas. Our brilliant educators and thinkers, global and local, had so much to offer and we wanted to make those ideas more globally accessible. To that end, we are introducing *KOLOT: Celebrating the Plurality of Jewish Voices*, a new journal created to expand the conversation to all interested in creating a deeper and more pluralistic Jewish community.

This project has been a labor of love and I would like to thank all who helped transform *KOLOT* from dream to printed piece. I would like to express my gratitude to our talented VBM *KOLOT* Editor Ginette Daniels for her tremendous erudition and leadership making the first VBM journal possible. I'd like to thank Abraham J. Frost for his creative design, editing, and publishing work. And, of course, I'd like to thank all of my colleagues who submitted such thoughtful material for this journal. Visioning never happens in a vacuum and I am very grateful to our dedicated and strategic VBM Board of Directors: Stan Hammerman (Chair), Mark Feldman (Treasurer), Judi Gottschalk, Josh Wertlieb, Dr. Jeffrey Packer, Leslie Goldman, and Sam Saks. Further, none of this would be possible without VBM Founder Rabbi Darren Kleinberg having demonstrated the wisdom and perseverance to found this great organization.

Thank you all for your support helping us in building our very special VBM community. Together, we are doing our part to enable the Jewish people to survive and thrive and we are bringing the wisdom and light of our tradition to the world.

Rabbi Dr. Shmuly Yanklowitz
Executive Director – Valley Beit Midrash

KOLOT
Table of Contents

Dear Reader,

Welcome to the first edition of *KOLOT: Celebrating the Plurality of Jewish Voices*.

Valley Beit Midrash (VBM) was established in 2007 with the singular goal of improving the quality of Jewish life in the Greater Phoenix Jewish community. The best way I knew how to do that was through the medium of Jewish education. Undoubtedly, there are other vital paths to a rich and meaningful Jewish experience, but education was the path that brought me to Jewish life and I wanted to share that with others.

Thankfully, my vision was shared with extraordinary leaders in the community, from both the lay and professional ranks. After six years, VBM was engaging more Jews in serious Jewish learning than any other organization between Texas and California. The addition of the Start Me Up! Fellowship (and the projects it would seed), the VBM Teen Scholars Program, and HaRofeh: The Jewish Medical Society of the Valley only served to increase the impact of VBM. These were the joint accomplishments of countless volunteers, donors, organizational leaders, and thousands of individuals that participated in our programs. Thank you.

When I decided to take the post at Kehillah, I knew that Rabbi Dr. Shmuly Yanklowitz would be able to continue the important work of VBM and broaden its scope beyond my own vision. This publication is just one example that my intuitions were correct. This journal means that VBM will have an impact that reaches far beyond the Greater Phoenix Jewish community. If Rabbi Shmuly's previous accomplishments are any indicator, I trust that this journal will be read in communities all over the world.

Congratulations to Rabbi Shmuly, Ginette Daniels, the leadership of VBM, and the Greater Phoenix Jewish community on this wonderful achievement.

Rabbi Darren Kleinberg
Founder – Valley Beit Midrash

Rabbi Darren Kleinberg is Head of School at Kehillah Jewish High School in Palo Alto, CA. He was the founding executive director of Valley Beit Midrash.

Ordained in 2005, Rabbi Kleinberg is currently completing his doctoral thesis, entitled *Hybrid Judaism: Irving Greenberg and the Encounter with American Jewish Identity*.

From Ginette Daniels
Senior Editor
KOLOT

To our Readers:

Welcome. I am honored and privileged to introduce you to our premiere issue of *KOLOT: Celebrating the Plurality of Jewish Voices*, a publication of Valley Beit Midrash (VBM).

At VBM, we believe that that our diverse Jewish voices should be heard and that we all have a stake in creating our Jewish future. We also believe that the more inclusive, transparent and authentic the conversation, the stronger – and closer – our community. Closer does not mean all-of-a-piece; it means respect for divergent opinions knowing that the sum is greater than any of the already amazing parts. All we ask is that we are of like mind when it comes to embracing our differences and growing stronger from them Our contributors to this inaugural issue come from near and far both, geographically and spiritually. Some have been our VBM partners from the start. Some are nationally known scholars, teachers and thinkers such as Rabbi Bradley Shavit Artson, Rabbi Dr. Yitz Greenberg and Anita Diamant. We are honored to have them all share the wisdom of their voices.

Our first issue tackles the very essence of our Judaism and how it inspires us. We have asked each contributor to ponder this statement: *"I am Jewish and I believe in the power of...."* Our responses reflect the depth – and variety – of our Judaism and the passion of our contributors. For some, their journeys are highly personal; for others, they derive their strength from the power of prayer, traditional Jewish observance, social action, Israel, music, history, learning, camp, interfaith connections, social justice and the belief that we are all *B'tzelem Elohim*. All are a part of why we are so proud to be Jews and why we dedicate ourselves to making a difference, however we define it. In future issues of *KOLOT*, we will explore the subjects introduced here in more depth.

If you are active in your faith, if you lost your connection, if you are new to Judaism, or just plain curious, however you come to these articles, we ask you to take a fresh look at each response. Do they resonate with you? Do you take issue? Do you feel inspired? How would you answer the question we posed to our contributors? And then, if something in what you have read has touched your heart, make just one commitment to put your ideas into words and your words into action.

Inspired by the contributions of our authors, I will get us started with my personal response:

I am Jewish and I believe in the power of our ancestors: I am Rachel bat Moshe v'Semha. My friends call me Ginette. Born of a Sephardi mother and an Ashkenazi father, and proud and humbled to have as part of my family tree – our ancestors Avraham, Yitzchak, Yaacov, Sarah, Rivka, Leah and Rachel, as well as my great grandfather Hai Joseph Cohen ben Zion, a respected rabbi from Algeria, my great uncle Ernest Cohen who died at Auschwitz with his entire family, my grandfather Reuben Furman, who struggled to bring his family from Odessa to the Bronx and made his life as a tailor. I know I can always be with them, as they are all within me, deep in my heart.

I am Jewish and I believe in the power of prayer: Although I was raised in an unorthodox way spiritually, exploring other religions first, I did not really connect to my Jewish roots till I joined Temple Chai in Phoenix, AZ. Today, as I stand and pray, what never ceases to fill me with the awe and the power of our faith is that I know that Jews everywhere have been saying these same prayers, no matter where they call home.

I am Jewish and I believe in the power of community: I am part of *Klal Yisrael,* a community that cares for each other through good times and bad. A community that has welcomed me and has become my extended family. I am nourished by the Hasidic joy of Rabbi Levi Yitzchak of Berdichev, by the philosophic search for truth of Maimonides and by the Zionism of Theodore Herzl.

I am Jewish and I believe in the power of tradition. I place the Lord before me always, *Shiviti Adonai le negdi tamid,* when I sing the wordless melody of a *niggun,* when I chant the ancient words of Torah, when I touch the mezuzah, when I taste the challah on Shabbat, when I pray for those in need of healing, when I give *tzedakah,* whenever I kindle the divine spark within me and let it blaze with a love of Hashem and a pursuit of holiness.

I am Jewish and I believe in the power of our faith: My Judaism is my inner compass: guiding me to pursue righteousness, goodness, justice and love; reminding me to be thankful for my blessings, turning my focus away from myself and towards others; and reintroducing me to the joy of life.

I am Jewish and I believe in the power of answering God's call: I will never forget the words of my Rabbi and mentor, Bill Berk, who said that it is a great joy and a great burden being a Jew. That it is easy to be there for those we love, for our family, but we also must be there for our community, when the Jewish people call out for our help. And if we are, one day that burden will become the greatest privilege of our lives. We will know in our hearts that we can't say no; that we must say yes. So, when called, I will answer as our ancestors, did: *hineni*, Here I Am. I know that God is calling and I must be there to make a difference for our people, in whatever way I can, because I am Jewish.

Now it's your turn. We want to hear from you. Please contact us at **VBMKOLOT@gmail.com** for possible consideration for future issues.

Ginette Daniels is Senior Editor for Valley Beit Midrash's new publication: *KOLOT: Celebrating the Plurality of Jewish Voices*. She is also a lay leader and spiritual educator at Temple Chai and founder of the Temple's SOUL Brigade, an inspired corps of lay leaders trained to support clergy.

This year, she launched a new spiritual program called The *Art of Living Wisely: An Eight-Fold Path*. The program, based on a multi-faith approach to wisdom teachings and practices, gives spiritual seekers the tools they need to connect to their inner selves and their communities. Ginette is the co-author of *Safe at Last in God's Shadow: A Life in Search of the Divine*.

The Power of Learning, Leading and Prayer

Rabbi Dr. Shmuly Yanklowitz
Executive Director
Valley Beit Midrash

Do you feel vigorously alive each day? Or, must you "bleed just to know you're alive?"

Rabbi Jonathan Sacks, in *A Letter in the Scroll*, offered a remarkable insight into the traditional Jewish psyche: "Jews were always a tiny people, yet our ancestors survived by believing that eternity is found in the simple lives of ordinary human beings. They found God in homes, families and relationships." As Rabbi Sacks wrote, the Jewish religion proposes that simply turning on our souls can connect us to a miraculous existence.

I have encountered too many people who wait to truly live their lives. Many wait until retirement, or "when life is less busy"; unfortunately, by then, the ability to live fully has tragically been drained from the soul. Living fully cannot, indeed should not, be put on hold. The mind and soul are instruments that must be constantly played to keep the music alive.

Meditation and prayer are, of course, vehicles to light our souls. Prayer needs to emanate from our being and be meaningful, not just the thoughtless recitation of static liturgy. The great rabbi and philosopher Bahya Ibn Paquda, also known as Rabbeinu Bachya, wrote: "Prayer without *kavanah* (spiritual focus) is like a body without a soul." Similarly, the renowned Maimonides taught: "True *kavanah* means freedom from all extraneous thought and complete awareness of the self within the greater presence of the Divine."

Consider the advice of the great American poet Mary Oliver, in her poem "Praying:"

It doesn't have to be
the blue iris, it could be
weeds in a vacant lot, or a few
small stones; just
pay attention, then patch
a few words together and don't try
to make them elaborate, this isn't
a contest but the doorway
into thanks, and a silence in which
another voice may speak.

It is a perpetual struggle, and we must always work to instill in ourselves this imperfect yearning. We cannot lapse into a rhythmic and rote routine, but must approach prayer with a sense of wonder and amazement at the beauty and meaning of what we are doing. Max Planck, the architect of quantum theory, explained his perspective regarding scientific inquiry:

> The feeling of wonderment is the source and inexhaustible fountainhead of the desire for knowledge. It drives the child irresistibly on to solve the mystery, and if in his attempt he encounters a causal relationship, he will not tire of repeating the same experiment ten times – a hundred times – in order to taste the thrill of discovery over and over again. The reason why the adult no longer wonders is not because he has solved the riddle of life, but because he has grown accustomed to the laws governing this world picture. But the problem of why these particular laws, and no others, hold, remains for him just as amazing and inexplicable as for the child. He who does not comprehend this situation, misconstrues its profound significance, and he who has reached the stage where he no longer wonders about anything, merely demonstrates that he has lost the art of reflective reasoning (*Scientific Biography*, 1949, 91-93).

Just as Planck explains how age and routine make us lose our sense of wonder, the same applies with prayer and meditation. We simply grow accustomed and too familiar with the process, the words, and the actions. However, as Planck says, the wonder and amazement still exists, in fact it abounds. We are just misunderstanding and not fully comprehending the situation – we are "misconstru[ing] its profound significance."

"We rise in solidarity when we help others rise. Each moment provides this holy opportunity and we must not forsake that."

We must endeavor to keep the ideals of our religion, of our prayers, and of our learning alive, regardless of this challenge. The philosopher Susan Neiman writes that keeping ideals alive can oftentimes seem a losing battle, an unattainable goal that can cause great distress, but human dignity requires the love of our ideals:

> Keeping ideals alive is much harder than dismissing them, for it guarantees a lifetime of dissatisfaction. Ideals are like horizons – goals toward which you can move but never actually attain. Human dignity requires the love of deals for their own sake, but nothing guarantees that the love will be requited. You might fail to reach your object, all your life long (*Moral Clarity*, 159).

The honored academic and former politician Michael Ignatieff has suggested, in an article published in the *New York Times Magazine*, that it is idealism (as opposed to relativism) that has made the United States a unique country:

> A relativist America is properly inconceivable. Leave relativism, complexity and realism to other nations. America is the last nation left whose citizens don't laugh out loud when their leader asks God to bless the country and further its mighty work of freedom. It is the last country with a mission, a mandate and a dream, as old as its founders. All of this may be dangerous, even delusional, but it is also unavoidable. It is impossible to think of America without these properties of self-belief.

The Jewish people, much like America, are a people of immutable ideals. We are a people who have upheld these ideals for thousands of years and have endured vicious, hateful, and murderous persecution because of our steadfastness and refusal to turn from then.

Our devotion to idealism sets us apart and we must never shy away from it; instead, we must wear it as a badge of courageous honor and imbue our ideals in our actions.

However, we must also maintain self-awareness. The British psychiatrist Maurice Nicoll described the capacity for self-invisibility and human blindness:

> We can all see another person's body directly. We see the lips moving, the eyes opening and shutting, the lines of the mouth and face changing, and the body expressing itself as a whole in action. The person himself is invisible... If the invisible side of people were discerned as easily as the visible side we would live in a new humanity. As we are we living in visible humanity, a humanity of appearances...All our thoughts, emotions, feelings, imaginations, reveries, dreams, fantasies are invisible. All that belongs to our scheming, planning secrets, ambitions, all our hopes, fears, doubts, perplexities, all our affections, speculations, ponderings, vacuities, uncertainties, all our desires, longings, appetites, sensations, our likes, dislikes, aversions, attractions, loves and hates – all are themselves invisible. They constitute "one's self" (*Living Time*, 3).

Religion can help with this process. Marx's famous line dismissing religion as the worthless "opiate of the masses" has been taken out of context over time. In fact, Marx was actually describing the enormously powerful influence and ubiquity of religion. Consider the line in its context:

> Religion is the general theory of the world, its encyclopedia, its logic in popular form, its spiritual *point d'honneur*, its enthusiasm, its moral sanction, its solemn complement, and the general ground for the consummation and justification of this world... Religious suffering is at once the expression of real suffering and the protest against real suffering. Religion is the sigh of the oppressed creature, the heart of the heartless world, just as it is the spirit of spiritless people. It is the opium of the people (*A Contribution to the Critique of Hegel's Philosophy of Right*).

One of the crucial aspects of religion is that we do not simply engage in private spirituality but rather engage with the power of interconnected synergistic striving – that of collective covenant. While interacting and sharing our religious traditions and practices within a community, we affect each other deeply and come to grow together. Political journalist Theodore White described how a piece of metal and a block of gold, when held together, will invisibly exchange molecules with each other, in the same way people share parts of themselves with others:

> When people are pressed close, they act the same way.
> Part of you enters them, part of them enters you. It is
> humbling and frightening to think that every person
> you've hated, or feared, or ran away from, or even
> loved is now a part of you. It is humbling and exacting
> to know that by our merely being together over the
> years, throughout close proximity, something happens
> within us that even science cannot describe (*The
> Mountain Road*, 340-1).

One of the by-products of communal interaction and support is the inspiration of deeper thinking and encouraged creativity. Yet, even in solitude and aloneness, man is creative, endowed with independent thinking and ingenuity. From the beginning of time, humans have always had creative potential, even in isolation. Rabbi Yose taught about how the first man, Adam, acted creatively to breed mules:

> Two things entered the thoughts [of God] to be created
> on *erev* Shabbos, but were not created until the
> departure of Shabbos. At the departure of Shabbos, He
> placed in Adam understanding reflective of the Divine
> model. And [as a result] Adam brought two stones and
> ground them together, and flame shot out from them.
> He brought two animals [a horse and a donkey] and
> crossbred them, and a mule issued from them (*Pesachim*
> 54a).

"Through learning, leading, and prayer, we have such an incredible opportunity to reach new levels within ourselves and embrace the light that burns inside."

The teaching from Rabbi Yose relates to the more fundamental question of how people function within societies and learn. For centuries, philosophers and laymen have been debating the merits and weaknesses regarding learning collectively as compared with learning independently. The famed, classically liberal philosopher John Locke argued that one should be educated within the norms of community, whereas Jean-Jacques Rousseau argued that one should be isolated from the norms of the community, since each individual is unique and requires his/her own development according to his/her inherent nature.

Rousseau makes a very important point in his position, that one must be oneself. The Kotzker Rebbe (Menachem Mendel) taught that one of the most spiritually poisonous types of religious life is to engage in activity because someone else does it or because it is one's own routine. On the other hand, as Jews, we understand the power of community and of habitual ritual. We can and must find opportunities to support each other, lift each other to new spiritual heights, and help each other learn and grow. One of the greatest gifts we can ever give others is to light their spiritual fire and inspire them to fulfill their life purpose. In each encounter, we have the choice and power to lower another or to raise them up! We rise in solidarity when we help others rise. Each moment provides this holy opportunity and we must not forsake that.

In all we do, we must strive to be fully engaged, ever mindful of the meaningfulness of our actions, and cognizant of the power we have to lift our brothers and sisters to new heights. Through learning, leading, and prayer, we have such an incredible opportunity to reach new levels within ourselves and embrace the light that burns inside. We must cultivate that light to truly live. There is no need to wait until we have more time, more money, and fewer responsibilities; as Rabbi Sacks suggested, all we must do is turn our souls on and we will instantaneously connect to the marvelous. It is my prayer that we live each day with open hearts, open minds, and open souls, ever aware of others and ourselves.

Rabbi Dr. Shmuly Yanklowitz is the Executive Director of the Valley Beit Midrash. He completed a Master's Degree at Yeshiva University in Jewish Philosophy, a Master's Degree at Harvard University in Moral Psychology and a Doctorate at Columbia University in Epistemology and Moral Development.

Rav Shmuly is the author of six books on Jewish ethics and was listed as one of *Newsweek*'s America's Top 50 Rabbis.

The Power of Unity Within Community

Rabbi Pinchas Allouche
Congregation Beth Tefillah

Winds of uncertainty are blowing across the globe. The future remains unsure. Will the sun shine again? Will stability reemerge after the storm dies down?

Jewish communities worldwide are also suffering their own turbulent storms. As some grapple to find answers to the many unanswered questions, the curse of division hovers. To paraphrase Jonathan Swift, the eighteenth century Anglo-Irish satirist: "We have just enough religion to make us hate one another, but not enough to make us love one another."

So how should we proceed? What can we do, individually and communally? How can we fruitfully direct our efforts and our community down paths toward to a better, stronger and healthier future?

A decade ago, researchers in this country asked a large group of people whom they would turn to if they needed help.

"Our first step toward a better future must be a collective rededication to one another."

The results were astounding: While a small percentage said they would turn to a government agency, 86 percent said they would seek out a member of their religious congregation. Perhaps this is but an expression of our intrinsic interdependence. Human beings yearn for one another; we need each other. It is no coincidence that in the entire book of Genesis only one thing is called not good (*lo tov*): "It is not good for man to be alone."

As a rabbi, one of my deepest pleasures stem from the silent observations I enjoy making every week. As in many communities, we at Beth Tefillah are abuzz with activity on the holy day of *Shabbat*. Chants of *mazel tov* are sung for babies recently born and couples just married. Warm wishes are offered to our fellow congregants in need of healing, and words of comfort are bestowed upon the mourners. It is particularly these moments of life and love that fill me with true *nachat* and satisfaction, for they stand as a reminder that, ultimately, it is this unbreakable sense of community that empowers and uplifts us to a place where no challenge is too big, no obstacle too tall.

> **"It is this unbreakable sense of community that empowers and uplifts us to a place where no challenge is too big, no obstacle too tall."**

Hence, our first step toward a better future must be a collective rededication to one another. Lend an attentive ear, extend a helping hand, reach out with a genuine smile. We must be there for each other. Not because of a relationship of power or honor. Not for self-serving reasons or purposes. But simply because it is indeed "not good for man to be alone."

My dear mentor, Rabbi Adin Steinsaltz, once shared with me that the difference between a wise man and a fool is that a wise man "makes the important issues of life important and the trivial issues trivial." Conversely, a fool "makes the important issues trivial, and the trivial issues important." These statements best summarize the vital approach we must undertake. True, we differ in many ways, and our perspectives are at times sharply different, but in the end, we must make our common "important issues" important, and let the trivial ones find their proper place.

After all, what unites us is so much greater than what divides us: We all desire to make the world a better place. We all strive to become true lights unto the nations. We all endeavor to nurture our children and surroundings with the teachings of our Torah. We all care deeply about our communities, and we all wish to actualize their endless potential and harness their dynamic force.

Yet, we can only do so if we learn to maintain a sense of proportion between the important issues and the trivial ones and direct our focus on the former only. If we have visions and plans of action for the benefit of our communities, we must work together to make them important and worthy of attention. This will build bridges, not walls; love, not apathy; harmony, not dissonance.

Finally, we must remember that Judaism has forever taught

that we are what we do. The more we engage in actions of goodness and kindness, the more we become good and kind. It is no secret that so much more can be accomplished with silent actions, small or big, than with loud words. If we each take upon ourselves to act more and say less, one *mitzvah* at a time, one good deed at a time, one soul at a time, our communities will undoubtedly become the model of goodness they so strives to be.

Rabbi Pinchas Allouche is the spiritual leader of Congregation Beth Tefillah in Scottsdale, Arizona, where he resides with his wife and eight children. He is a respected rabbinic figure, a sought-after lecturer, and author of many essays on Jewish faith, mysticism and social criticism. From 1999 until 2002, Rabbi Allouche served as a teacher and educator in the Mekor Chaim School in Jerusalem and in the Jerusalem Seminaries for young Jewish Women, Torat Chesed and Tikva. Prior to joining the greater Phoenix community, Rabbi Allouche served as a Rabbi, Youth and Programming Director, in Congregation Beth Tefillah of Atlanta, Georgia.

Besides his academic pedigree, Rabbi Allouche is highly respected and tremendously involved in the Jewish community of Greater Phoenix. He is a member of the Think Tank Committee of the Jewish Federation of Greater Phoenix, and he teaches middle school Judaics at the Pardes Jewish Day School. Rabbi Allouche is also member of the Vaad Harabanim, and the Orthodox Rabbinic Council - Arizona's Committee of Orthodox Rabbis.

In 2013, Rabbi Allouche was listed in the *Jewish Daily Forward* as one of America's 36 Most Inspiring Rabbis, who are shaping twenty-first century Judaism. Rabbi Allouche is also a blogger for the *Huffington Post*, *Times of Israel* and other publications.

The Power of Love

Rabbi Bradley Shavit Artson
Dean's Chair at the Ziegler School of Rabbinic Studies
American Jewish University

Recently, I received a package in the mail from Professor Thomas Oord, a Christian theologian who teaches at Northwest Nazarene University in Idaho. He mailed me two of his latest books because he read an article of mine and he thought they would help us launch a conversation. The two books offer an extended argument that the central virtue of Christianity ought to be love. Not faith, not salvation, but love. Reading his insightful books (*Defining Love* and *The Nature of Love: A Theology*) it occurred to me that the subject is one that has a natural home in Judaism, and calls for a Jewish reclamation. I want to make an argument for why love is important as a Jew; what it is that Jewish love looks like, and how we might resolve to attempt a more persistent and resilient love to heal this broken world and to bring wholeness to shattered hearts.

I do not need to tell you that this is a brutal age. All you have to do is peruse the news to know that this era reels from gruesome violence; that vast civilian populations are terrorized in every sector of the globe; at home the political system is stymied by rampant partisan viciousness, as Democrats and Republicans have lost the ability to learn from each other, and instead they caricature each other, yelling invectives from across the aisle.

We witness examples of humanity's inhumanity in all regions of the globe: so called "honor" killings, terrorism so prevalent that the newspapers no longer use that word to describe the people who assault innocents and who murder children. Slavery, which we once thought was relegated to the nineteenth century, is now practiced in most parts of the world, especially victimizing children and women. There is ubiquitous sexual predation; we see bigotry based on orientation, or faith, or skin color, or ethnicity, or place of origin.

The list goes on and on of people assaulted by the violence of others. As a result, countless people feel increasingly lonely, lacking in community, lacking in belonging, and lacking in meaning. The cycle spirals out: the more people fear, the more they give into hate. The more vulnerable they feel, the more they hate. The more ruthless and unconnected, the greater their rage and hatred. Adrift in meaninglessness, they confuse hatred for purpose, and multitudes cling to their desperate disdain of those they don't really know as a way of anesthetizing their own fragility. Extremists feed on that fear and desperation. They suck strength from the way people feel assaulted, misunderstood, or at risk, causing people to feel further victimized. The cycle begins again.

"The need for love - strong and abiding - is so pressing because the hatred is so great. Judaism's response to hatred has always been to redouble our efforts at love."

We Jews know that same reality from our own history, both ancient and recent. We are told that we were slaves in Egypt and outcasts; we know that we were to the Egyptian overlords *to'evot* – abominations – and so we caricatured them as idolaters and they caricatured us as degraded. We construed our encounter with Egypt as a cosmic battle between good and evil. Throughout our ages there has been an endless series of people who have beaten, raped, and murdered Jews simply for being Jews, and that same anti-Semitic distortion and violence continues in our own time around the world; I believe, especially, the level of hatred against the State of Israel and calls for its destruction can only be characterized as insane. Meanwhile, we Jews also make choices that contribute to the victimization of others even as we attempt to transcend our own victimization.

We need to talk about love. The need for love – strong and abiding – is so pressing because hatred is so great. Judaism's response to hatred has always been to redouble our efforts at love. To be able to love more persistently than those who hate; more resiliently than they fear, to answer acts of violence with acts of resolute justice, to be able to stand for values of righteousness and decency and inclusion in places of terror and of fear, and of exclusion. It is time to reclaim *chesed*, covenantal love, as the imperative of this age, and to assert *chesed* as the central Jewish religious value.

Love is the Antidote to Hate

Why is love the antidote to fear and to hate? Scripture tells us: *"olam chesed yibanei* – I will build this world with love" (Psalm 89:3). The cosmic and biological force for building a new and a better world is love. Supernovae give off their core to spawn new generations of galaxies and to forge the elements that make life possible. Life clambers toward complexity and consciousness by transmitting love and life to new generations of life. Mammalian parents cradling their young understand the redemptive power of love. Children clasping the arms of an elderly grandparent understand the redemptive power of love. Every one of us – in churches, synagogues, mosques and temples – read lyrical liturgical poems of love; the secular and religious alike soar to the creative efforts of artists across the centuries who share their love in music, sculpture, drama, and words.

Only when people feel valued, recognized and affirmed, only then can we take the risk to see the humanity of the people around us. Jewish tradition understands that insight and cherishes knowing that God has chosen us; this is what gives the Jewish people resilience, generosity, and fortitude. It is only through love that we can, in fact, become open to the needs of other people to affirm their humanity, however much they may belittle their own. There is a story of is one of the great Hassidic rabbis in the late 1700s, a man named Rebbe Moshe Lieb Erblich, known as a Sassover Rav:

> The Sassover Rebbe enters an inn, and sits beside two local peasants. As the two peasants sit at the bar and drink, they begin to fall into a drunken stupor. One turns to his comrade and says, "Tell me, friend, do you love me?" His colleague responds, "Of course I love you. We're drinking companions. Naturally I love you." Then the first one said to his friend, "Then tell me, friend, what causes me pain?" His colleague said, "How should I know what hurts you? I'm just your drinking buddy." He said, "If you loved me you would know what causes me pain."

It is told that from that day on, every time the Sassover Rebbe taught, he taught his students that to love another human being means to know what causes them pain, to know what makes them suffer, to know what makes them hurt. And it is a small step from knowing what causes someone's heart to break, to feeling mobilized to do something to alleviate pain.

Another story about the Sassover Rebbe:

> It is told that on the holiest day of the year, Yom Kippur, the Sassover's congregants were sitting in the *shul* waiting for the services to start - but no rabbi. One woman decided that she was close enough to her home that she could leave the synagogue quickly, check in on her child, make sure that he was safe and comfortable, and then she could rush back; no one would notice. She ran home, opened the door to her hut, and there, sitting next to her child's crib, was the rabbi, cradling the sleeping child in his arms. He looked up at her and said, "I was rushing to get to *shul* on time, and I heard crying coming from your house. As I entered the house I saw that your child was awake and scared. So I rocked him in my arms and we sang together until he fell asleep. By then I had forgotten what day it is today."

What kind of a great tradition tells a story about a rabbi who forgets that is it Yom Kippur? What an amazing heritage recounts the tale of a *tzaddik*, one of the righteous, who thinks that rocking a baby to sleep is more important than leading services? What a poignant and wise pathway to understand that it is in holding each other, in singing together, that we fashion the kind of world in which we aspire to live. Perhaps that is why *Shir Ha-Shirim* – the greatest love song of all time (and the book the ancient rabbis tell us the Bible's most sacred) – teaches us "love is as strong as death, and as mighty as *sheol*."

In an age teeming with merchants of death, in an age in which there are people who seek to impose a living hell on their fellow human beings, we must respond with a redoubled *ahavah*: redoubled love.

We must love stronger than they hate. We must love longer than they hate. We must teach them that our *chesed* will draw out their poison.

What Kind of Love Can Save?

It is said that one can tell a lot about a culture by its vocabulary. I cannot speak the Eskimo languages, so I can't verify the popular claim that Eskimos have dozens of word for snow. But I do know that we Jews have inherited many ways to say love. I have already utilized the first:

Ahavah – simply love
Achvah – the kind of fraternal brother/sister love that one feels for someone who understands your soul
Rachamim – a kind of love that comes from the word *rechem*, a womb. It is a mothering love, and we even affirm that mother-love is so important that the Talmud refers to God as *Rachamana*, the womb-like one who births new worlds
Chafetz – desire, as in *"mi-ha-ish heh-hafaytz chaim,* who is the person who desires life?"
Ratzah – will, as in Yehi ratzon ... may it be your will, Lord our God, to grant us a sweet and a happy year
Hedvah – passion
Reut – friendship
Chibah – longing, yearning
Chashak – desire
Yedid – beloved
Chanan – sweetness
Chesed – most frequently mentioned of all, is lovingkindness.

Permit me to point out an interesting characteristic about *chesed*, and in fact, about all of these loves. They do not refer simply to internal feelings. They are not just a kind of emotion. If all you do is feel a warm burning in your heart, swallow some antacids, lie down, and the feeling will go away. Love is not love if it does not generate empathy, well wishes, and deeds of lovingkindness. That is why the Bible almost always precedes the word *chesed* with the verb, *oseh*, to do. *Chesed* is not merely something you feel, *chesed* is something you do for the people you love. Judaism understands love to be covenantal — the dynamic and persistent integration of the inner emotion/virtues of affection, empathy, desire, yearning and delight with deeds of *tzedek* (justice), *shalom* (wholeness/integrity), and *berakhah* (blessing/wellbeing).

Chesed is covenantal; it is always about relationship. Love takes place between two parties, not internally within a single individual. *Chesed* is dynamic, meaning it is always changing, open to integrating new insights from the world and the covenantal partner; and it is persistent. Love does not back down; it neither retreats nor surrenders; and *chesed* integrates and harmonizes emotions and behavior, specifically the emotions of affection, empathy, desire, yearning, and delight with three great offerings of deed: the rubrics of *tzedek*/justice, of *shalom*/peace, and of well being/*berakhah*.

Chesed is Covenantal

That definition is a mouthful, and it will reward us to analyze its component parts in turn. Jewish Love is covenantal. Covenants are not necessarily restricted to equal parties. Kings and vassals are not equal, yet they provide the sociopolitical context for the biblical covenant. God and the Jewish People do not claim to be equal, but they do insist on the ability to bridge the chasm of disparity with relationship, and in relationship one may stand as a partner even with someone who is not your equal. Love spans that gulf, and non-equals are able to stand in partnership and in dignity together, despite their differences and perhaps because of their distinctiveness. Our entire tradition is a recurrent outpouring of covenantal love, so that God creates the world in order to have an object to love. As if that isn't enough, God rises up against Pharaoh and brings us to freedom, because God so loves our ancestors. And then as if that is not enough, God brings us to the foot of Mt. Sinai, and there offers us a covenantal contract, which the rabbis tell us is a *Ketubah*, a wedding contract. The wedding contract sealing the relationship between the Jewish people and God is the very *Sefer* Torah.

Ours is an ancient tradition of covenantal love. And strikingly, covenantal love is very different than popular culture's portrayal of love, in which love is the pitter-patter of a heart, but that pitter-patter only lasts as long as it takes to cook a pop-tart. Five minutes later, our attention drifts to some other infatuation. So we live in a culture with all these romances, passionate beginnings and frequent flammable finales. We read about the various stars and their love affairs, and we can read about their breakups and their new love affairs. That superficial, provisional appetite is not covenantal love. Covenantal love, we are told, nurtures understanding and generosity: seeing the best in your lover, seeing the best in your children, in your community, in humanity, in the world and then with similar generosity, sharing in their struggles; sharing in their efforts.

Such covenantal love is both dynamic and

"In a world in which some go to bed hungry, some go to bed impoverished, some go to bed sick or lonely, we Jews are commanded to know what makes them hurt, and we are commanded to lift them up."

persistent. Love is sometimes misunderstood as a fleeting passion. Even worse, it can be taken to be a cool intellectual assessment of value. Between the incinerating heat of passion and the icy chill of assessment, there is no room for a love that lives. Jewish love is alive, which means it's always open to change. As the philosopher Franz Rosenzweig reminds us, "Love brings to life whatever is dead around us."

Nobody can be in a relationship without being open to change. Ask any parent, and they will affirm that what it means to be a child's parent is different now than it was a year ago. And it will be different, thank God, a year hence. Love alters when it finds alteration - a responsive vulnerability, but it must also be persistent. When your child presents you with a challenge, it is your love that will sustain the child, providing the strength to overcome. It is that yearning for life, for wholeness, and for connection that allows us to withstand life's disappointments, pains, and brutality. Our enemies do not understand this. They rely on force. They rely on fear. They rely on terror. These traits are static and they shatter from their brittleness. But love, expressed diligently and persistently, will wear them down.

Chesed is the integration of values and emotions with deeds. One of the defining characteristics of every living creature is homeostasis, the ability to maintain a consistent, internal environment despite an external environment that changes. That ability to integrate is the hallmark both of being alive and of having character. Love is the ability to integrate all our powerful emotions and in consistent empathic behavior. Our emotions inspire us to act. Our actions hone and habituate our feelings. The cycle is never static and never ending. The cascade of feeling to behavior to elevated feeling to ennobled behavior spirals us toward infinity. "I love (*ahavat*) you, says God, with an everlasting love, therefore I continue my lovingkindness (*chesed*) to you (Jeremiah 31:2)."

Love (*ahavah*) ripens as lovingkindness (*chesed*), primarily in three clusters: The first is *tzedek*, justice. The symbol of *tzedek* is the scale evenly, tentatively balanced. Judaism understands that love and justice are not conflicting values. They are dual expressions of one core value, as light is both particle and wave. Indeed, Judaism affirms that love is the source and the root from which nourishes justice, while justice is the fruit and the flower of determined, abiding love. Jewish tradition reminds us, "You shall not oppress a stranger, for you know the feelings of a stranger, having yourselves been strangers in the land of Egypt (Exodus 23:9)." Sage advice attributed to Philo, an ancient Jewish philosopher: "Be kind, for everyone you meet is fighting a great battle." We know that *chesed* results in acts of caring and justice. Covenant love is not weak: it does not tolerate a world in which there are no rules, no consequences. *Chesed* is resolute, strong, insistent, and fair. But it is, above all, love.

The second great cluster is *shalom*, which is understood as peace, but it means so much more. Shalom comes from the Hebrew word, *shalem*, which means wholeness, integrity. Baruch Spinoza wrote, "Peace is not the absence of war; it is a virtue, a state of mind, a disposition for benevolence, confidence, justice." Love must be grounded in the entirety of who we are - our memories, character, experiences, body, temperament and aspirations. And our love must be grounded in our integrity – in the authentic selves we are in private and public. As the Hasidic master, Rabbi Simcha Bunim told his students, "You cannot find peace anywhere if you do not find it in yourself." The wholeness and integrity of shalom means not making yourself small because others would have you shrink from your own greatness. *Shleimut*, wholeness, means offering to the world the fullness of who you are at your best: your beauty as you are, your greatness as you are. That *shleimut* means inviting others to rise similarly to their unique greatness. Jewish tradition understands that the value of *Shalom* is an act of love so significant, that it is nothing less than messianic. It will advance the age of universal harmony if we practice *shleimut* with resolute determination: "If you fulfill the law of kindness to birds, you will fulfill also the law of freeing the slaves … and you will thereby hasten the advent of the coming messiah (*Deuteronomy Rabbah* 6:7)."

"Judaism affirms that love is the source and the root from which nourishes justice, while justice is the fruit and the flower of determined, abiding love."

Finally, the third great cluster is the value of *Berakhah* – of blessing and well-being. There is so much bounty manifest in this world, a harvest that we did nothing to deserve. We were simply born into a world that was prepared across the millennia for our arrival. Our task in the world is to savor the bounty, to delight in it, to steward it, and to help each other to do the same. We make of ourselves a blessing and commit to being grateful for the blessings. That is why the structure of Jewish prayer always starts *Baruch Attah*. *Baruch*, in the blessing formula, does not mean blessed literally. God does not need our blessing. God is the Source of all blessing, the fount of all bounty. So we start our *berakhah*, our spur to mindfulness by noting: You, God, are bountiful, *baruch Attah*. After that general admission we then specify God's particular lovingkindness of that occasion: You are bountiful for giving us Torah… You are bountiful for giving us life and bringing us to this season… You are bountiful for giving us bread to eat. Jewish prayer is a resilient discipline reminding ourselves of the bounty of being alive, and that we are called to embody God's image. We are called to be like God, sources of bounty and blessing for others: "Be a blessing… and in you shall all the families of the earth be blessed (Genesis 12:2)."

In a world so afraid that it routinely erupts in hatred, we are commanded to love. In a world in which children go to sleep without knowing that they are safe, or that there will be a meal tomorrow, we Jews are commanded to love. In a world in which people believe they can bully the State of Israel out of existence, we are commanded to stand tall for the liberation and national self-expression of all peoples, and to love. In a world in which some go to bed hungry, some go to bed impoverished, some go to bed sick or lonely, we Jews are commanded to know what makes them hurt, and we are commanded to lift them up.

At this precious moment of new beginnings, I bless us all that we feel in our hearts the resilient power of *chesed*, of *rachamim*, of *ahavah*, of love, and then, knowing that we are loved with an eternal love, we roll up our sleeves and return to the task of healing this cruel and beautiful world.

Rabbi Dr. Bradley Shavit Artson (www.bradartson.com) holds the Abner and Roslyn Goldstine Dean's Chair of the Ziegler School of Rabbinic Studies and is Vice President of American Jewish University in Los Angeles. Further, he is a member of the Department of Philosophy. Rabbi Shavit's primary academic interests are theology, ethics, and the integration of science and religion. He supervises the Miller Introduction to Judaism Program and mentors Camp Ramah in California.

Rabbi Shavit is also dean of the Zacharias Frankel College in Potsdam, Germany, ordaining rabbis for the European Union. A regular columnist for the *Huffington Post* and for the *Times of Israel*, he is the author of 10 books and over 250 articles, most recently *God of Becoming & Relationship: The Dynamic Nature of Process Theology* (Jewish Lights).

The Power of Jewish History

Dr. Lawrence D. Bell
Executive Director
Arizona Jewish Historical Society

Jews and History/History and Narrative

The discipline of history involves the documentation of our past in a chronological, temporal manner, and the study of that past through empirical analysis of original and independent sources. The word "history" is derived from the Greek word "historia" (ἰστορία), meaning learning by inquiry and narrative. Because traditional Judaism often maintains a religious and transcendental explanation for our past (for example: the reading of the Haggadah at Pesach which is the reliving of the Biblical story of Exodus through each generation), the study of Jewish history as a discipline is a relatively recent phenomenon.

Prior to modern times, when Jews did turn to history as a tool for documenting and explaining our past, it was generally during times of crisis. It was the rebel-turned-Roman historian Josephus who recounted the story of the war with Rome (66-73 CE) and the terrible sacrifice at Masada. During the Crusades, Jews used historical chronicles to describe the chilling waves of massacre and ritual suicide as bands of crusaders ransacked the Jewish communities of the Rhineland in 1096 and again in 1147. In our own times, we have embraced history to document the systematic degradation, expulsion, and murder of our people during the Holocaust. Without the tools of history (empirical research and the use of independent primary sources) we would not be able to know who was killed and how; where they died and when; nor would be able to make this information available to others in an incontrovertible way. "He who controls the present controls the past. He who controls the past controls the future." These Orwellian words were intended to describe the

"In many ways, the study of Jewish history is the chart of this interaction - between the Jewish people and our religion - over time."

frightening falsification of history by the totalitarian regimes of the twentieth century. Yet, they also speak to its enormous power to shape our minds, our lives, and our identity. It is the past that inspires the future and it is in the past that we can seek our own future in a time of social fluidity and rapid technological change.

At its root, history is about narrative. It is about creating a story of real, lived experiences as they unfold over time. As such history offers enormous creative potential to those who are seize it. One example of this potential is found in modern Zionism. Like all modern nationalist movements, Zionism was built upon history, and the interpretation of a historical narrative that explained and cultivated the common experiences of the Jewish people over time. In their case, the founders of Zionism decried the degeneration of the Jewish people in the Diaspora and called for our restoration in the ancient Hebrew land of Israel. Although their inspiration came from the Bible, it was historical rather than religious in nature, viewing the Jewish past not in miraculous terms, but as a linear progression through time to be changed and altered by human action. From this vision of history, a nation-state was born.

The Potential of History for Jewish Identity Today

Can the study of Jewish history sustain Jewish identity in the twenty-first century? This is difficult to answer, but history certainly can serve as a valuable tool in shaping Jewish religious, social, and community life. For identity to be perpetuated, it must continually re-engage multiple generations, and history has the potential to do that. Moreover, history can appeal to those Jews who do not belong to congregations, but who still identify as Jewish and seek a meaningful participation in Jewish community life. In this manner, the study of Jewish history can accentuate religious Judaism rather than distract from it. History can be a portal, a point of access to the larger Jewish world. It can also provide context for understanding our religion and the means by which it developed.

This, in fact, was my own experience. Growing up as a young man, I first became interested in Judaism, truly interested, through history. At a time when I did not yet have the spiritual maturity to appreciate our religion, I was able to interact with my heritage mainly by studying history. These studies helped to define my own self-identity and I soon decided to make a career of it by becoming a Jewish historian. The study of Jewish history taught me how a Jewish community works and how our communities have served the needs of Jews throughout different times and places. Jewish history also prompted me to consider such questions as the future of Jewish life in America and nature of our relationship with the larger society. If it had not been for Jewish history and the academic pursuit of Jewish studies, I would likely not have entered Jewish community life or understood my own responsibility for engaging and perpetuating Jewish identity.

In addition, the study of history can teach us important lessons about the nature of time. We often get too wrapped up in the ever-changing flutter of the present. If we are to build a foundation for a strong future, however, we must dig deeper into the continuities of our past. The great French historian Fernand Braudel once explained that history has three levels: the *événement*, or the fluctuations of day to day events; the conjuncture, the deeper social and economic patterns that underlay these events; and finally the structure, or *longue durée*, which exposes the great fault lines and fissures over which the human experience transpires. What this layered concept of time can teach us is that even in periods of rapid change, the continuities of history persist, and continue to shape us in ways in which we are not always aware. Everything that takes place in the present has a context in the past.

Our long experience has shown that Jewish identity is rooted in God, the Torah, and Israel. Yet while our religion itself may be transcendent, religion also requires people in order to become realized. In many ways, the study of Jewish history is the chart of this interaction - between the Jewish people and our religion - over time. Jewish history also reveals how Jews in the past responded to times of prosperity and times of persecution, how we have adapted and innovated, while at the same time retaining the core elements of our identity over thousands of years.

The experiences of the twentieth century created great disruptions for Jewish life and Jewish identity. The destruction of the core European Jewish communities in the Holocaust left the Jews of Israel and the Americas as the torchbearers for a world our forefathers left behind. As a result, we have become disconnected from our immediate Jewish past to an extent not seen in hundreds of years. This is found in our religious practice, community life, and social interactions.

"History can be a portal, a point of access to the larger Jewish world." We find ourselves in a period of profound anxiety and cultural malaise as our last connections to the older world of European Jewry disappear. How do we perpetuate the memory of that which has been lost? This question has no answer. We cannot bring back the lost communities of Europe. We can only move forward in time.

We must realize that we have not lost the threads of our deep past, just our immediate past. By looking back beyond our immediate past, we may actually be able to gain insights for looking forward. History can offer some suggestions. The co-existence of Babylonian Jewry with the Second Temple Judaism somewhat parallels today's situation with Israel and the United States. The integration of Jews in Roman society or during the Golden Age of Spain can yield clues for how to survive, indeed thrive, over multiple generations in an open, friendly, and fluid society. Our history has always been an ongoing creative process. Instead of lamenting our situation, let us embrace it: How might we in the United States adapt the experiences of our deeper Jewish past to the uniquely American environment of freedom and mobility in which we live? The study of Jewish history clearly provides insight as we grapple with the challenges of a new century.

Dr. Lawrence Bell
received his Bachelor's Degree in History from Arizona State University and his Master's and Ph.D Degrees in Jewish History from The Ohio State University.

In addition, Dr. Bell also has extensive occupational experience in archival management. He has served as the Executive Director of the Arizona Jewish Historical Society, part of the Cutler✿Plotkin Jewish Heritage Center, since 2005.

The Power of Israel to Renew Our Judaism

Rabbi Bill Berk
Rabbi Emeritus
Temple Chai

Perhaps, the biggest story in Israel is the power story. For two millennia, Jews lived in places where they were, for the most part, powerless. Now, since 1948, we have been living with power. We were out of practice and much of our contemporary history is about the struggle to learn to use power well. But there's another power story that is much harder to grasp. It's the power of Israel to re-shape our Judaism.

As I see it, these are the big ideas of Zionism:

- Jews need to stop relying on supernatural power – they can do this by re-entering history, which means re-entering the world of natural power
- Jews are a people and, as such, need to all be able to go into the same tent
- Zionism will put an end to anti-Semitism
- By returning home and building a Jewish state, we can once again become a light to the nations.

Zionism enhances our sense of what it means to be a Jew. (Or, Zionism might bring a new and larger sense of mission and dignity that we will need to discover and enact—a mission that will include redrawing the boundaries between the secular and the religious and the national and the religious).

These last two "big ideas" suggest the promise of a new Judaism; I believe in the power of Israel to help us renew our Judaism. After all, we have not had a Jewish country in two thousand years and it makes sense that once we did, everything would be different – including our Judaism, how we think about God, *mitzvot*, *halakha*, and how we "do Jewish."

Rabbi Abraham Joshua Heschel wrote that: "We have not even begun to fathom the meaning of this great event [the return of the Jewish people to their homeland]" (*Israel, An Echo of Eternity*, 219).

Someone who did a lot of thinking about the meaning of this great event is Rabbi David Hartman. He writes:

> "The land of Israel is holy from the covenantal perspective because it invites greater responsibility and initiative on the part of the community. It is the framework in which ways must be found to make the Torah a viable way of life for a community… I live with the guarded hope that out of this complex and vibrant new Jewish reality will emerge new spiritual directions for the way Judaism will be lived in the modern world. Israel expands the possible range of *halakhic* involvement in human affairs beyond the circumscribed borders of home and synagogue to the public domain. Jews in Israel are given the opportunity to bring economic, social, and political issues into the center of their religious consciousness" (*A Living Covenant*, 283-4).

This expanding Judaism might just be the biggest story unfolding in Israel. You see it in the little green shoots of native Israeli spirituality coming forth from the country's rock music and our poetry. You see it in the "post-secular" Israel that is emerging, as there are more and more "secular" yeshivas built and secular synagogues, secular *Kabbalat Shabbat* services on the beach or on kibbutzim. You see it in the religious identity crisis that has touched all Israelis, including, finally, our Haredi (ultra-Orthodox) brothers and sisters. All you have to do is check out the number of Haredim entering the army, the university, and high-tech jobs and you realize that something big is happening. You see it in the army's code of ethical conduct that leans on our tradition and on what Yitzchak Rabin called "the shards of Jewish memory" to formulate new *halakha* about how modern armies need to operate. You see it in the debates in Israel where the values of our Torah often shape the contour of the discussion – such as the issues around health care and housing and the safety net. You hear it in the magic of the Hebrew language – language that carries with it such power, grace, memory, cultural insights, and traditional values.

For me, the impact of Israel on my Judaism centers on the power of experiencing Jewish public space and

"We have not had a Jewish country in two thousand years and it makes sense that once we did, everything would be different – including our Judaism, how we think about God, *mitzvot, halakha,* and how we 'do Jewish.'"

Jewish public time. At the grocery store, a week before Passover, I heard a clerk singing one of my favorite Passover songs (*Ve-he She-amdah*). It hit me – Passover penetrates the street, the market place, the culture. I had no idea how beautiful Shabbat was until I experienced a "Jerusalem Shabbat." I did not fully get the transformational influence of Shabbat until I witnessed, week after week, this city of 804,000 people utterly transform itself every Friday afternoon. What was a religious culture suddenly becomes something larger—beyond religion. When Jews visit Israel they often get this—they see their Judaism on a larger screen, on a bigger stage and it inspires them. Their spiritual/religious journey is then shaped by this experience.

As David Hartman argues, Jewish sovereignty gives us the opportunity to expand our Judaism. There is no guarantee that we will succeed. There are forces determined to change nothing. As I see it, the change is already happening. There are new traditions and new kinds of Jews. The stories and poetry and liturgies that the kibbutz movement produced have not vanished. They pop up wherever you find Jews, rooted in our land, struggling to do what Hayim Nahman Bialik said we would do – revive our land, our language, our state. New Torah is emerging from all the tumult of this third Jewish commonwealth. That is the power of this place and it is the most exciting thing that's happened to us in a very long time.

Rabbi Bill Berk was ordained at the Hebrew Union College in Cincinnati where he won awards in homiletics and social action.

Rabbi Berk served for 23 years as the Senior Rabbi of Temple Chai in Phoenix, Arizona. During his time there, Temple Chai grew from a congregation of 80 families to a community of 1,120 families. Rabbi Berk did pioneering work in the area of recovery prayer and Kabbalat Shabbat, adult learning, assisting Jews with special needs, developing the caring/healing congregation, and using retreats to strengthen community. In 2003, he won the Covenant Award given to the three top Jewish educators in North America.

From 2004-2010, Rabbi Berk was the director of the Center for Rabbinic Enrichment for the Shalom Hartman Institute in Jerusalem. In 2010, he joined Keshet, The Center for Educational Tourism as an educational consultant, tour educator, marketing coordinator and director of Keshet's bar/bat mizvah trip programs. He made to Israel in 2006 and is currently Rabbi Emeritus for Temple Chai. He is married to Batya and has five children.

The Power of *B'tzelem Elohim*

Rabbi Micah Caplan
Congregation Or Tzion

In my humble opinion, the most effective way to express being
Jewish is by taking our Jewish learning and transferring it into
Jewish living. We can learn about what it means to be charitable
and make the world a better place through the values of *tzedakah*
and *tikkun olam*, but then it is up to us to take the texts that teach us
such values and bring them to life through being charitable and
just, doing what we can to transform our surroundings for the
betterment of society.

There are many Jewish values rooted in the Torah
(including *tzedakah*) that have had a tremendous impact on the
world and that on a personal level, I believe in. And, it is rather
difficult to choose only one that has had and continues to have a
deep impact on my personal being. We each might have our own
Torah value that is closest to our heart that if asked, we could put
in the form of a bumper sticker. So, if you were asked what you
believe in as the Jewish value that you believe in the most, which
would it be?

For me, I believe in the power of *B'tzelem Elohim*, the text
found in the first book of the Torah, the Book of Genesis. In the
first chapter, we read that the human being was created *B'tzelem
Elohim*, which some translate as "in God's image." I like to
translate this text to read, "fashioned with a godly image." The
idea that each human being is endowed with godliness is so
meaningful, so crucial and so important in defining how we need
to treat one another. The "concept" that each of us has a piece of
God within provides tremendous power and direction as to how
we are to treat one another, no matter our religion, culture or
ethnicity.

When we look at others and at ourselves in a godly
manner, we bring sanctity and humility to our world in a very

"The 'concept' that each of us has a piece of God within provides tremendous power and direction as to how we are to treat one another, no matter our religion, culture or ethnicity."

special way. The Torah teaches us "from the beginning" that each person is divine, that each individual is unique, that each soul is precious. The Torah's phrase "*B'tzelem Elohim*, fashioned in a Godly way," means that we carry the potential to reflect the divinity within each of us. I believe in the power of *B'tzelem Elohim* because it is the source of all other actions, words, relationships and realities that we create for ourselves, towards others and with God.

If we enable *B'tzelem Elohim* to have such an impact, and if we believe in its power, then all of the other texts, values, morals and lessons that we treasure will fall into place and have their own and equal impact on the world.

.

Rabbi Micah Caplan joined Congregation Or Chadash in the summer of 2010. He has long-standing ties to Phoenix having grown up here where his father served as Cantor and mother as Musical Director of Har Zion Congregation. Rabbi Caplan has led large congregations in Florida and California where he introduced exciting adult learning and youth programming. Under Rabbi Caplan's leadership, the Or Chadash community grew from 110 to 400 families. His vision is creating a place of learning, sharing and celebrating Jewish living together as a Kehillah Kedosha – a holy community. He is known for his warm, personal outreach.

In May of 2014, Congregation Or Chadash merged with Har Zion Congregation to form Or Tzion, where Rabbi Caplan serves as rabbi of the congregation. Rabbi Caplan and his wife Michelle are the proud parents of three beautiful children: Brianah, Julia, and Avi.

The Power of Prayer

Rabbi Mari Chernow
Senior Rabbi
Temple Chai

In an essay entitled "The Spirit of Jewish Prayer," Abraham Joshua Heschel worried that modern Jewish prayer was in danger of losing its vivacity. He regretted the loss of elements such as fervor, authenticity and grace. He asked, "What is grace?" and responded, "The presence of the soul. A person has grace when the throbbing of his heart is audible in his voice; when the longings of his soul animate his face..."[1] Heschel critiqued prayer that felt sober and staid, "Now, how do people pray? They recite the prayer book as if it were last week's newspaper...No one knows how to shed a tear. No one is ready to invest a sigh. Is there no tear in their souls?"

I believe in the power of prayer because I am certain that there is a tear in every soul. Indeed, I am certain that we have the capacity to pray with the passion and the immediacy that Heschel so succinctly demanded. I believe in the power of prayer because who has not known the distress and relief that comes simultaneously when we can no longer prevent our hearts from throbbing in our throats? Prayer is a haven for our fiercest and most urgent emotions.

Author and liturgist Catherine Madsen calls for a vocabulary of prayer that is enduring and alive. She urges us not to discard ancient tropes that feel irrelevant, but rather to revisit them through a contemporary lens. Modeling just that, she urges us to learn "to speak once again as accurately as possible the language of broken heartedness and ardor and fear...a profound language of prayer is intrinsic... it is not too hard for us, neither is it far off, but already in our mouths and in our hearts." In other words, the *siddur* should come to life in the hands of the person who prays. If we are able to think and feel - and we are able to think and feel - then we possess

---

[1] *Moral Grandeur and Spiritual Audacity*, 102

possess the building blocks for a serious and passionate prayer life. Madsen focuses on broken-heartedness, ardor and fear, but Jewish prayer also expresses despair, delight, gratitude, grace, wanting, wishing and much more. As we experience the peaks, the valleys, and everything in between, prayer reflects and re-shapes our responses. I myself have prayed the words of the broken-hearted, the ardent, the fearful, the emboldened, the anxious, the disappointed, the inspired, those who have been granted reprieve and those who are struggling to forgive. I believe in the power of their prayers and, too, in the power of mine.

 Prayer should open the gates of emotional honesty and probing introspection. Even though Jewish prayer is fundamentally communal, it must nurture realizations that are personal and private. Prayer brings us to truth telling. To pray is to affirm that our own lives are worthy of reflection. I turn again to Heschel, who reflects on his experience of Kol Nidre and the emotions it provoked: "It would be a great calamity for humanity if the sense of embarrassment disappeared, if everybody was an all-rightnik, with an answer to every problem. We have no answer to ultimate problems. We really don't know. In this not knowing, in this sense of embarrassment, lies the key to opening wells of creativity."[2]

 For those who yearn for such creativity, a considerable challenge to prayer can be our relationship to the *siddur*. If I open the prayer book to any page, it's possible I may find a statement of faith I do not believe, a miracle I do not think could happen, or an idea I simply do not like. For the sages who composed and compiled it long ago, the words were urgent and immediate. But are their passions ours? If prayer is truth telling, how do we relate to a prayer book that seems ungrounded in what we normally recognize as truth?

 Singer and songwriter Ani Difranco answers a similar question in the language of her Christian tradition. She writes:

---

[2] *Moral Grandeur and Spiritual Audacity*, 147

When they said he could walk on water/
What it sounds like to me/
Is he could float like a butterfly/
And sting like a bee. (*Verses*)

Here, she suggests that although centuries of Christian interpreters have read a passage as being literal, the modern Christian is free to read it as metaphor. So too, of course, for Jewish texts and prayers. Metaphor is an entrée into meaning and magnitude. Consider these verses:

- We are like a fleeting wind, our days like a passing shadow[3]
- You roll light away from darkness and darkness from light[4]
- You spread a shelter of peace over us[5]
- Remember us and write us into the book of life, the book of merit, the book of compassion and forgiveness[6]
- Let the field and all that is in it sing for joy[7]
- Let every tree of the forest arise in delight. Let justice roll down like waters and righteousness like a mighty stream.[8]

Madsen encourages us to set aside "intellectual processing" and rather aim for "emotional ingestion" of the poetry of prayer. We do not reject William Blake simply because we cannot literally see a world in a grain of sand or hold eternity in an hour. Rather, we emotionally ingest the startling beauty of timelessness. Anyone who has ever felt a lifetime of meaning in a fleeting flash knows that what Blake writes is true even if it is not true. So too, for those who desperately need to know that the darkness will eventually peel away or those who are imaginative enough to dream up the tranquil serenity that would exist underneath God's shelter of peace, prayer speaks the truth. I believe in the poetry of prayer.

---

[3] Psalm 144:4
[4] Ma'ariv Aravim
[5] Hashkiveinu
[6] Avinu Malkeinu
[7] Psalm 96:11-12
[8] Amos 5:24

Prayer language will not always be easy. Certain liturgies have modified difficult language in order to make it more palatable. In so doing, they have risked sacrificing the fire, the intensity, and the disquiet that we need prayer to provoke. I share the concern of Madsen who writes, for example, about figurative interpretations of the Unetaneh Tokef of the High Holy Days. She is unsatisfied by lines such as, "When we really begin a new year it is decided. And when we actually repent it is determined. Who shall be merely alive and who shall exist. Who shall be happy and who miserable." She criticizes "the softening of the essential point that we do not know the hour or manner of our death. By recasting each kind of death as a metaphor of personal growth, the prayer replaces the horror of contingency with the self-absorption of neurosis – as if fire and water had ceased to be lethal, as if hunger and thirst were obsolete, as if there were no plague worse than the pressures of conformity" (CM 19).

In its raw and penetrating nature, *Unetaneh Tokef* forces us to confront and cope with a reality that is all but impossible to accept. Even as we desperately pray for events to turn our way, by praying we acknowledge that we have no way to ensure that they will. Prayer is, or should be, humble acknowledgement of our lack of control. Life is absurd. Loss is absurd. We can do nothing to change that.

The liturgy should challenge us, but the individual praying always has the right to edit and omit. One of the very first appointments I had as a rabbi was with a man whose son had tragically died. He came to ask me about the very sentiment that Madsen defends in *Unetaneh Tokef*. How was he to pray during the upcoming High Holy Days to God who determines "who shall live and who shall die." My answer was, "Maybe you don't. Not this year. Not until you are ready. Maybe not ever. You have other sentiments to express - let those be your High Holy Day prayer." Prayer may help us express pain that is already there but not create resentments and regrets of its own.

So too, we should feel comfortable adding original words. There will be days when the language of the *siddur*, as beautiful and provocative as it is, does not suffice. That's why there is always room for spontaneous and personal prayer. That's why new prayers will always continue to be written.

Consider this selection from Leonard Cohen's *Book of Mercy*:

> Like an unborn infant swimming to be born, like a
> woman counting breath in the spasms of labor, I
> yearn for you. Like a fish pulled to the minnow, the
> angler to the point of line and water, I am fixed in a
> strict demand, O king of absolute unity. What must I
> do to sweeten this expectancy, to rescue hope from
> the scorn of my enemy? The child is born into your
> world, the fish is fed and the fisherman too.
> Bathsheba lies with David, apes come down from the
> Tower of Babel, but in my heart an ape sees the
> beauty bathing. From every side of Hell is my greed
> affirmed. O shield of Abraham, affirm my
> hopefulness.

I believe in the power of provocative, evocative language that must be read (and prayed) again and again. But having devoted most of this essay to the importance of words, I will turn briefly in conclusion to the importance of music. As Zalman Schacter Shalomi wrote:

> Most of the time, on most levels of our being, we live
> in the prosaic world. In prayer we want to shift our
> center of gravity toward the right brain, to feel closer
> to the soul-unfolding that *davening* can bring. We can
> do that through enchantment – en-chant-ment,
> singing ourselves into a different way of being.

It is daunting for many of us to consider singing with abandon, singing out loud, singing so that others will hear. But a great release of the soul comes when we are bold enough to do so – to sing our hearts out, to sing in defiance, to sing as a sign of resistance and resilience, to sing out the absurdity of our lives, to sing in amazement and glory, to sing while we march and build and plant and pray for social justice, to sing in harmony or cacophony, to sing, to sing, to sing.

For these reasons, I believe in the power of Jewish prayer.

Rabbi Mari Chernow has served as a leader of Temple Chai since 2003. She graduated from University of California, San Diego and was ordained from the Los Angeles campus of the Hebrew Union College. She studies regularly at the Shalom Hartman Institute where she completed the Rabbinic Leadership Initiative in 2010. She has also taken courses with the National Outdoor Leadership School, the Mussar Institute, the Institute for Jewish Spirituality and Arizona State University's graduate program in Counseling. She has served o n the Board of Overseers of HUC-LA, the Reform Movement Think Tank and the Board of Directors of Pardes Jewish Day School.

Rabbi Chernow is passionate about Jewish learning, prayer and healing. She enjoys skiing, surfing and rock climbing, none of which compare to the delight she experiences when enjoying her family.

The Power of Optimism

Anita Diamant
Best-selling Author and Journalist

According to that famous Chinese proverb, "It is a curse to live in interesting times." So we're good, because "interesting" doesn't begin to describe what we're living in. These are extraordinary times for lots of reasons, but chief among them is the dizzying rate of change that is taking us, well, we have no idea where. And we all know it isn't likely to slow down. This can be disorienting. But a curse? No. There has never been a better time to be Jewish. Not for me and not for my daughter.

Not everyone agrees that these are the good times. There are Jews who see nothing but threats on the horizon. They advise us to circle the wagons and they presume that survival depends upon our elites, like Rabbi Shammai, who said, "One should teach only one who is wise and humble of good family and rich." If I quote Shammai you know what's coming next: Rabbi Hillel said, "Teach everyone." Hillel rejected litmus tests for wealth, family name, and wisdom, even humility. In other words, even the dull and arrogant had a place in his classroom. "Teach everyone," Hillel said, "because there were many sinners in Israel who were brought near to God by studying Torah and from whom descended righteous, pious and honorable people." Rabbi Joseph Telushkin, in his wonderful short biography of *Hillel: If Not Now, When*, says that not only was Hillel arguably Judaism's greatest rabbinic sage, he was also its most fearlessly inclusive.

Telushkin writes: "What shines through the teachings of Hillel and his disciples is a fundamental optimism about human nature and the capacity of Torah to affect people positively.... If Torah has something to teach the world, its message shouldn't be restricted." Rabbi Hillel also said, "The highly impatient person cannot teach." He believed that, as important as it is for teachers to know their material, it is even more important to love what they teach and to love their students.

Teachers should embody the Golden Rule. What is hateful to you, do not do to your student: no showboating for the sake of demonstrating how learned you are. Show respect by teaching to the level of your students.

Hillel said, "Teach everyone." I would add, "Teach for the beginner, but also, teach with a beginner's mind."

This does not mean dumbing down. Indeed, it means staying in touch with the amazement and awe of learning Torah for the first time. It means thinking outside the *bimah*, moving outside the comfort zone of the yeshiva. It means remembering that someone in your classroom does not know the meaning of the words *bimah* or *yeshiva*.

When you do not translate *bimah*, which means pulpit, you close a door just a little bit. When you do not explain that yeshiva refers to a place of serious Jewish learning, you add a few more grains of sand to a stumbling block you cannot see. This is understandable. After years of hard work to earn your degree, you may well have forgotten what it's like to be a beginner.

Translate everything. This is not just for the benefit of new Jews or non-Jewish spouses and in-laws, friends and guests. This is for the benefit of Jews you think understand. It's taken me thirty-five years as an adult Jewish learner to ask for translations without being ashamed.

Everyone is a beginner in some area of Torah, a word with onion-like layers of meaning. The dictionary definition of torah is: instruction or teaching. The Torah refers to the first five books of the Hebrew Bible, but Torah also refers to all sacred and religious literature: the whole bible, Talmud and all of the later commentaries, the writings of the mystics, Jewish philosophy, and liturgy.

Torah, however, is even more expansive than that, encompassing all Jewish thought. Including Purim Torah, which includes equal parts terrible jokes, pun-filled plays, song parodies and silly sermons. We can speak with urgency about a Torah of the planet Earth. Physics has given us a Torah of unified field theory.

A Torah of social justice includes the biblical prophets and the history of Jewish involvement in the American labor and civil rights movements.

There is the Torah of Kushner, not just Rabbi Harold or Rabbi Lawrence, my teacher. But also Tony Kushner, the esteemed playwright, who put the entire *Kaddish* prayer, which is recited in memory of the dead, in Aramaic, smack in the middle of *Angels in America*, the Pulitzer Prize winning classic of the contemporary American stage.

There is the Torah of Jon Stewart, who I consider the chief rabbi of the United States or, if you prefer, our leading prophet, speaking truth to power with a punch line.

Too far out? Too on the fringe? Hey, if you don't have fringes on the corners of your *tallis*, your prayer shawl, you're wearing a tablecloth. It's all about the fringes.

Our Torah is oceanic, with room for Hillel and Shammai, physics and physical comedy. We are all beginners.

So, teach Torah to everyone. Teach to beginners and cultivate a beginners mind as you teach the Torah of *menschlichkeit*, of being a good person; the Torah of *B'tzelem Elohim*, of the radical equality of all human beings fashioned in the image of the divine; the Torah of *tikkun olam*, of responsibility and politics.

I share Hillel's fundamental optimism about human nature and about the vitality of our vast and elastic tradition that can infuse daily life with meaning, beauty and holiness when we sit in the classroom and when we meet at Starbucks; when we stand up for what we believe in, and when we bend low to comfort the fallen; when we walk down Boylston Street, and when we're watching television, when we study together and, I pray, whenever you teach your Torah.

Now, go change the world.

Anita Diamant is the author of eleven books. Her first novel, *The Red Tent*, published in 1997, won the 2001 Booksense Book of the Year Award. A bestseller in the US, it has been published in more than 25 countries. She has also written three other novels: *Good Harbor*, *The Last Days of Dogtown*, and *Day After Night*.

Diamant has also written six non-fiction guides to contemporary Jewish life, including *The New Jewish Wedding*, *Choosing a Jewish Life* and *The New Jewish Baby Book to Saying Kaddish*. An award-winning journalist, she graduated from Washington University in St. Louis with a degree in comparative literature and holds a Master's degree in English from Binghamton University. She is founding president of Mayyim Hayyim: Living Waters Community Mikveh, a twenty-first century reinvention of the ritual bath, making an ancient ritual available and responsive to the needs of the entire Jewish community.

This piece is based on Ms. Diamant's June 2013 commencement address at Hebrew College in Newton, MA. Ms. Diamant was awarded an honorary doctorate and asked to address the graduating class of educators, cantors and rabbis.

The Power of Intellectual Judaism

Rabbi Dr. Shmuly Yanklowitz
Executive Director
Valley Beit Midrash

Piety left the center stage of Jewish life with the destruction of the Temple, when we moved from a religion based around priestly rites to the academic, detailed, and all-encompassing structure of rabbinic Judaism. The paradigm shift not only moved our community from a religion centered on animal sacrifices to a religion of prayer and study: it was a transition from piousness to an intellectual, legalistic religion; Judaism came and proclaimed to the world that "Ideas matter."

Rabbi Shneur Zalman of Liadi, the author of the *Tanya* and founder of the Hasidic Chabad movement, taught that we have the spiritual power to bring ideas into existence:

> Whenever my master [Rabbi Dovber of Mezeritch], conceived an original [Torah] thought, he would voice it aloud, although those present could not understand him. He would speak as if to himself. By articulating the idea, he would draw it into this world. Once the idea was present in this world, it could occur to another person – even one at the other end of the world – who was laboring in the study of Torah and the service of God… Had it not been drawn into this world, even if the other were to toil mightily, he would not arrive at this idea – for it would still be in heaven (*Ma'amarei Admor Hazaken Haketzarim*, 474).

In the Baal HaTanya's view, we bring ideas into existence and they have great power once in this world. We are not merely concerned with simple meditations about peace. Rather, we must involve ourselves in complex ideas that matter in the world.

Some have lamented the so-called decline of the rabbi-as-intellectual. As rabbinical programs have become more focused on pastoral counseling, homiletics, social action, and management, intellectual pursuits have often fallen by the wayside.

"For the heart to be pure, it must be honest and critical; to dismiss big and important questions and concerns is to jeopardize one's spiritual health. When we live a life committed to ideas, we declare that we won't close our eyes to reality."

In modern times, Jews have a disproportionate number of secular intellectual accomplishments. For example, that Jews have won 18 percent of Nobel prizes despite only accounting for four-tenths of a percent of the world population. This success has not come because Jews are inherently smarter than everyone else; it only shows that the community is very intellectually engaged. Yet, why does that intellectual curiosity not always bridge over into the Jewish learning and discourse?

On college campuses, we see more young Jews interested in engaging lucrative careers in law, medicine, and commerce (all admittedly respectable) and a decline in pursuits of philosophy, literature, and the humanities. For example, among Yeshiva University graduates in 2011, accounting and general finance majors were nearly three times as numerous as Hebrew language and literature majors. However, it should be noted that, unlike national trends where business degrees were paramount and accounted for nearly one-fourth of total degrees issued in the United States, Yeshiva University graduates were most likely to have majored in psychology or biology than the business fields. This seeming paradox in Jewish intellectualism extends to the Ultra-Orthodox: Whereas Maimonides, the Jewish legalist par excellence, was also deeply engaged in philosophy, science, and other intellectual pursuits, the culture most engaged with Torah study today rejects altogether the value of secular study.

What's the value of an intellectual Judaism anyway? Why not just work hard, make money, donate, and spend the rest of our time in leisure with family and friends? Why should one be committed to lectures, books, classes, journals, and asking hard questions?

General trends in America may provide a warning to those who think this way. Reading at Risk, a 2002 Census Bureau survey of adults in the United States, reached this conclusion: "...literary reading in America is not only declining among all groups, but the rate of decline has accelerated, especially among the young." Among the reasons given is that while reading a book requires concentrated attention, Americans have increasingly turned to activities that "foster shorter attention spans and accelerated gratification." Furthermore, it portended ill for the future, as those who did not read were also less likely to be involved in political or cultural activities.

Among the findings of the report, comparing results in 2002 versus 1982, were:

- The share of Americans who read literature declined from nearly 57 percent to less than 47 percent, the first time in history that fewer than half of all Americans read books

- The number of those reading books of any kind declined by 4.3 percent

- Literary reading has declined at all education levels, including a drop of more than 15 percent in those who had completed college and graduate school, and 20 percent among those who had attended college

- In 2002, 43 percent of literary readers performed volunteer and charity work, versus 17 percent of non-literary readers.

(It should be noted that this survey took place before the arrival of Facebook, text messaging, and Twitter.)

Many have expressed the hope that eBooks would improve the situation. However, a December 2011 Pew Internet poll of adults recorded that more than half of U.S. adults reported having read five or fewer books (including eBooks) during the past year.

What are the consequences of this decline in reading and intellectualism? One result is that in an era of pundits on the airwaves, intellectuals and credentialed experts have lost influence. A century ago, Louis Brandeis, before his appointment to the Supreme Court, innovated the "Brandeis Brief" for court cases, incorporating sociological, demographic, economic, and legal data to form a compelling legal argument. During the New Deal, President Franklin D. Roosevelt employed a "Brain Trust" of Columbia University professors who worked on legislation that would promote economic growth. Today, however, many bloggers, talk show radio hosts, and cable news guests are more performer than intellectual. As a result, alarming numbers of Americans retain discredited conspiracy theories and other illogical fantasies.

Such deep-seated and erroneous beliefs have contributed to the complete paralysis of the federal government today. When you conceive your opponent as the devil, you are not going to engage in respectful behavior or move toward compromise. This is why climate change, the environment, poverty, and other critical issues remain ignored by certain sectors of the political elite.

Fortunately, we can act constructively by encouraging intellectual activities. Judaism teaches that *Rachmana liba ba'ei* – the Compassionate One, i.e. God, desires the heart. For the heart to be pure, it must be honest and critical; to dismiss big and important questions and concerns is to jeopardize one's spiritual health. When we live a life committed to ideas, we declare that we won't close our eyes to reality.

Jewish social justice depends upon a community that is attendant to the human condition, aware of contemporary social systems, well learned in Jewish texts, and critical in merging different systems of ideas. Maimonides goes so far as to argue that if we do not remove our own ignorance then we're at great risk of perpetuating evil in the world:

These great evils that come about between the human individuals who inflict them upon one another because of purposes, desires, opinions and beliefs, are all of them likewise consequent upon privation. For all of them derive from ignorance, I mean from a privation of knowledge. Just as a blind man, because of absence of sight, does not cease stumbling, being wounded, and also wounding others, because he has nobody to guide him on his way, the various sects of men—every individual according to the extent of his ignorance—does to himself and to others great evils from which individuals of the species suffer. If there were knowledge, whose relation to the human form is like that of the faculty of sight to the eye, they would refrain from doing any harm to themselves and to others (*Guide for the Perplexed*, 3:11).

Many Jews go on to get advanced secular degrees but remain childlike in their Jewish knowledge. How can someone take Judaism (or any religion) seriously if he/she has a child's education in it? To properly live a religious life, a Jew must not just rely on the education of his or her youth but continue to relearn the religion, and re-understand the Torah as he or she develops and society evolves.

Intellectual life is connected to spiritual life in this regard. Martin Buber explains the Baal Shem-Tov's teaching here:

The Baal Shem Tov teaches that no encounter with a being or a thing in the course of our life lacks a hidden significance.... If we neglect this spiritual substance sent across our path, if we think only in terms of momentary purposes, without developing a genuine relationship to the beings and things in whose life we ought to take part, as they in ours, then we shall ourselves be debarred from true, fulfilled existence (*The Way of Man*).

We have a precious legacy in our pursuit of intellectualism. As with other aspects of our tradition, true study requires discipline and concentrated attention, and a willingness to resist the constant use of text messaging, computer games, and other distractions. We know from our history that the rewards from these endeavors are great, and we can see around us the risks that come with neglecting them. Jewish intellectualism is not reserved for the elite. Rather, taking ideas seriously is an essential aspect for living a Jewish life.

The Power and Triumph of Life

Rabbi Dr. Irving (Yitz) Greenberg
President Emeritus
Jewish Life Network/Steinhardt Foundation

I believe with wholehearted faith that all human beings are created in the image of God and that they are endowed by their Creator with certain inalienable dignities among which are infinite value, equality and uniqueness.

I believe with wholehearted faith that poverty, hunger, oppression (including racism, sexism, anti-Semitism, slavery and all forms of systemized degradation), war, sickness and death are ultimately incompatible with the full dignity of the image of God. I believe with wholehearted faith that the human world cannot endure half slave and half free, half hungry and half fed, half neglected and half cared for, half human and half less than human. Therefore, the world must be made whole so that it will fully respect and sustain every image of God. We have a divine promise that this can be achieved.

I believe with wholehearted faith that all humans are endowed with the divine capacities such as power, consciousness, relationship, freedom and life. It is the task of religion and culture to lovingly help humans to perfect these qualities in imitation of God until the fullness of life is achieved.

The Call to Covenant

I believe with a wholehearted faith that out of love for all creation, out of respect for the dignity of humanity and out of longing for perfection, our loving God has summoned all humans to enter into a divine-human partnership to use their God-given capacities to perfect the world.

"I believe with a whole-hearted faith that out of love for all creation...God has summoned all humans to enter into a divine-human partnership..."

I believe with a wholehearted faith that, for both partners, entering into covenant is motivated by love. The validity of the covenant is based on the principle of free negotiations, mutual assumption of duties and full recognition of the equal rights of both parties. From the human perspective, joining the covenant involves the freely given and voluntarily accepted commitment of one's life and efforts to perfect the world.

I believe with a wholehearted faith that in entering into covenant, God fully accepts humans in their humanness. Therefore, the covenantal process of redemption moves at a human pace – typically one step at a time or as fast as people can grow and change. People start the cycle of love, care and equal treatment with their own immediate family, friends and community. Then this commitment is extended outward to the entire people and to the whole world.

I believe with a wholehearted faith that since the task of perfection cannot be accomplished in one generation, the covenant is ultimately a covenant between the generations as well as between God and humanity. Each generation is expected to move the world as far along the way to freedom and plenitude of being as it can. Each person is asked to respect the principles of the final perfection as much as they possibly can now. Each is asked not to take advantage of present privilege to hurt others, not to settle for the status quo, not to abdicate the task by escapism or by dismissing this world as illusion, not to allow the longing for perfection to so spin out of control as to lead to the destruction of what has been accomplished already. Each human is called to create and raise children (and/or to care for and educate others' children) so that they will grow up to be fully in the image of God and to transmit to them the task of perfecting the world. Thus, the chain of life will not be broken by death and the covenantal task will not be relinquished until the hopes of all are fulfilled.

The Limits of the Exercise of Freedom

I believe with a wholehearted faith that the covenantal mission should be pursued under conditions that fully respect every individual image of God. After all, if the means contradict the ends, the ends cannot be achieved.

Therefore, the covenant is based on freedom and the right to choose for one's self. The dignity of choice includes the right to be fully informed and educated, to freely associate with others, to create friendships, families and associations to advance every cause, to participate in selecting who shall lead in the tasks of life and government and society, to follow and practice the religion of one's choice, to voluntarily follow and learn from whatever models one chooses. All these freedoms must be exercised with full respect for one's own and one's fellow human beings' rights. Therefore, there should be covenantal restraints in all exercise of power, consciousness, relationship and freedom. These restraints are best accepted voluntarily but may be legitimately incorporated into law as well as into political, economic, social and legal structures.

"It is a time to work together to turn freedom, power and affluence into blessings for all."

I believe with a wholehearted faith that the Jewish people is called into covenant not by its own merit but by the gracious love of God; that Jews, individually and collectively, are chosen to serve as teachers, as models and as co-workers with humanity in the task of perfecting the world; that Jews have already served disproportionately and in distinguished fashion in these roles but that the task is not yet finished.

I believe with a wholehearted faith that other peoples, individually and collectively, are called not by their own merits but by the gracious love of God to be partners, to serve as teachers, models and co-workers in the covenantal task. All people, including Jews, should be allowed and helped to freely carry on their mission in mutual love and understanding. Everyone should be educated, inspired, corrected in accordance with their infinite dignity.

The Work of the Covenant Continues

I believe with a wholehearted faith that in this generation the Jewish people was totally assaulted with endless cruelty and put to mass death under conditions of systematic and total degradation. Yet, neither the people nor its divine partner yielded hope or lost faith in the promise of final perfection. Rather they renewed the covenant, increased life, reasserted the infinite value of each and every image of God, took power in the land of Israel and elsewhere to advance the cause of life and the dignity of human beings starting with their own but extending outward. By so doing, Jews renewed their classic role as teachers, models and co-workers. As is to be expected of human beings, Jews' behavior in these roles was flawed. But they have been worthy of their covenantal task which is yet unfinished.

I believe with a wholehearted faith that this is the appropriate time for all people to respond to the mass death and inflicted degradation of our time by increasing their efforts to perfect the world. This includes reviewing their own traditions, faiths, cultures, systems and institutions and, out of mutual love, removing all sources of hatred, indignity, denials of infinite value, equality and uniqueness of the other, intentional or unintentional. It is a time to work together to turn freedom, power and affluence into blessings for all. In this time, the Jewish people have a blessed opportunity to serve as a light unto the nations as well as to illuminate the example and inspiration of others. Acting together, this generation can make its contribution to ensure the final triumph of life.

Rabbi Irving "Yitz" Greenberg is President Emeritus Jewish Life Network/Steinhardt Foundation; President Emeritus, CLAL: The National Jewish Center for Learning and Leadership. Rabbi Greenberg is the author of the newly reissued, *The Jewish Way: Living the Holidays* (Touchstone).

This article was first published in the September 1993 issue of *Sh'ma: A Journal of Jewish Responsibility*.

The Power of Social Justice

Rabbi Ari Hart
Associate Rabbi
Hebrew Institute of Riverdale

During a steamy August in Chicago a few years back, I led a summer program called Or Tzedek that brought Jewish high school students to Chicago neighborhoods. Our goal was to explore Judaism and social justice. On the second day of the trip, I brought my students to Chicago's predominantly African-American southwest side. Our project for the day was knocking on doors and distributing leaflets to people in the neighborhood about prenatal health opportunities available to pregnant women.

On the van-ride down, some personal doubts emerged: "Why am I bringing these kids to this neighborhood? We're about to engage with an area and an issue that seem far removed from the Jewish people's agenda," I thought. "Is this really Jewish service?" The tension between universal social needs and personal and communal Jewish goals felt almost too much for the program to bear.

Those doubts lingered as our community partners described the health campaign. I deeply believed in the value of the project, but still I didn't see how the Jewish People had anything to do with it. I felt that perhaps as the director, I had strayed too far towards universalism and neglected the Jewishness of the program. Once we hit the streets however, my thoughts began to change.

We walked past a Baptist Church. I noticed a carving above the doorway – the Ten Commandments in Hebrew. Surprised, I looked closer, and saw in the doorway a space where a mezuzah had once been. It was an old *shul*, possibly the one my grandparents attended before they and the other thousands of Jews who lived on the south side fled to the suburbs, half a century ago. I pointed it out to some of the students, and a few of them shared that their grandparents too had lived in these neighborhoods, and perhaps had *davened* in this *shul*. Here, in an unlikely place, we found a deep connection to Jewish peoplehood through history and family. My "us-them" mentality shattered, as we began to feel a personal connection to the people around us.

The event gave my students an amazing opportunity to reflect on how they related to the Jews who formerly lived in this neighborhood, and to the residents of today. Did our families cause poverty here when they left? Are we now responsible for that today? How are our actions here today "Jewish"?

Interacting with the "other" can greatly sharpen our own identity. I realized that actions which appear to be thoroughly "non-Jewish" can be sources of tremendous Jewish import, meaning, and connection to Jewish peoplehood.

"It will take 'out of the box' applications of text, history, and values to forge the links between helping non-Jews and connecting to the Jewish people. We must bring discussions of Jewish peoplehood from conferences and boardrooms into the streets."

This is the challenge and opportunity of Jewish communal leaders today.

It will take "out of the box" applications of text, history, and values to forge the links between helping non-Jews and connecting to the Jewish people. We must bring discussions of Jewish peoplehood from conferences and boardrooms into the streets.

That's not to say that broad, social concerns do not dramatically affect our people already. The economic crisis of the last decade has resulted in a dramatic increase in the number of homeless Jews in America. In a globalized world, famine among wheat farmers in India will affect the price of *matzah* in Israel. American immigration policy affects the workers in Jewish slaughterhouses in Iowa. Government responsibility and disaster preparedness affects synagogues in New Orleans.

This challenge, to meaningfully fuse the universal with particular, goes both ways. For those of us who tend towards the particularistic side, we must strive to make links to the larger world. How do these issues affect us, and how do we affect them? What wisdom do we have to offer to the world's most difficult challenges? In addition, we must think about how the Jewish issues vital to our survival – Jewish poverty, anti-Semitism, preservation of culture and tradition, encouraging Jewish education, are mirrored and affected by the rest of the world.

What other people share our interests in preserving tradition and cultural norms? What other groups are fighting for return to homelands, or freedom of religious expression? How can we learn from them? How can they teach us about ourselves? Engaging deeply in these questions is not just a good thing to do – it thickens what Peoplehood is all about, making it more real, more meaningful, and more alive to millions of Jews.

For those of us who tend towards the universalistic, we must strive to create the ties back to the Jewish people in the issues and work we do in the world. What does the Talmud say about tenants' rights? How do Jewish farmers deal with modern environmental problems? How can we frame world issues using Jewish language, values, spiritual expression, and more? Who is the Jewish hero that inspires your work? How can we embed universalistic work inside a lifelong Jewish journey so it is not just another event, trip, not just another "experience"?

Tension usually connotes conflict and strife; tearing things and people apart. Tension can be constructive, however, even beautiful. Clever management of tension in bridges keeps gigantic structures aloft. The tension in violin strings produces the most beautiful melodies. The forces of universalism and particularism pulling at Jewish peoplehood are real. If we pull too hard in either direction, the Jewish people might snap and fragment. Let us continue to find that strong, beautiful balance between the universal and the particular, pushing our community to find ways of harmonizing what seems on the surface to be at odds, enabling ourselves to make our beautiful Jewish music for generations to come.

Rabbi Ari Hart is a leader of multiple initiatives that bring diverse communities together to make positive social change. Rabbi Hart is a founder of Uri L'Tzedek, the Jewish Muslim Volunteer Alliance and was the founding director of Or Tzedek, the Teen Institute for Social Justice in Chicago. He has led campaigns, taught and organized to spread the message of a powerful, prophetic Judaism that is a light for justice in the darkest corners of our world.

He currently serves as an associate rabbi at the Hebrew Institute of Riverdale, a leading modern, open Orthodox synagogue in the Bronx. A contributor to the *Jerusalem Post*, Al Jazeera, *Haaretz* magazine, the *Huffington Post*, the *Jewish Daily Forward*, he was recently selected by *Jewish Week* as one of the 36 "forward-thinking young people who are helping to remake the Jewish community." He was ordained by Yeshivat Chovevei Torah and studied in Jerusalem at Yeshivat HaKotel and in the Advanced Study Program at Machon Pardes.

The Spiritual Power of Jewish Music

Todd Herzog
Cantorial Soloist
Temple Solel

The fact that I am now a cantorial soloist at Temple Solel in Paradise Valley, Arizona, and a traveling Jewish musician comes as much of a surprise to me as it does to those who know me.

I was raised as a "typical" American Jew. I knew that I was Jewish. I went to my Nana's house on Passover and sat through the endlessly long seders. I went to Temple for the High Holidays, more out of responsibility than any kind of feeling of belonging. Jewish ritual in the home consisted of lighting candles on Chanukah and looking forward to the gifts each night. I didn't understand much about my religion or my culture.

When I was seven, my Mom visited Israel and came home feeling energized about her Jewish identity. She decided that I should have a more Jewish education. This consisted of Hebrew school on Tuesday and Thursday afternoons, starting in the fourth grade. Most of the kids in my class had been attending school since they were in kindergarten or earlier. I was always playing catch-up. There were two areas however that I loved and where I excelled: history and Hebrew language. I continued to study and became bar mitzvah, after which I informed my parents that I was "done" with Judaism. What I was learning was so far removed from my everyday life that I could not see the benefit of pursuing any kind of further study.

Socially, I felt alienated from Judaism as well. I attended a couple of youth group events but did not really connect with the kids. I never went to Jewish summer camp and still have not visited the land of Israel. However, ironically, looking back on my friends in high school and college, I still seem to have gravitated toward other Jewish kids – all of the guys in my high school rock band were Jewish and many of the guys with whom I sang with in my college a cappella group were Jewish as well. So, at some level, I must have been aware of our deeper cultural connection.

"I recognize that it is the music that has made me feel part of the Jewish community and that has given me a sense of my own identity as a Jewish man."

How did I end up where I am now? Was it fated? I can never know, all I do know is that it was not expected. Just after college, I dated a woman named Rachel who had just come through a bone marrow transplant. Interestingly, her dad is a cantor and Rachel had a very strong sense of Jewish identity. We were together for more than four years. During that time, she struggled with her health and finally suffered a relapse. Together, we went through several months seeking answers and trying a number of alternative treatments. It was during this time that I really began my quest for spirituality as a tool to understand what was happening in our lives. Unfortunately, Rachel ended up losing her battle with leukemia at age 28. My world was devastated. Everything I thought I knew about how life was supposed to work and how my own life would unfold evaporated.

I began to seek answers. I still did not connect any of those answers to Judaism. I considered myself "spiritual but not religious." I quit my job at the record label in Los Angeles where I had been working. I meditated, I wrote in my journals, I went for long hikes and sat by the ocean. I attained some level of peace, if not understanding. Still, it felt as though there was some piece of life that I was missing.

Fast-forward about five years when a woman named Karen from Phoenix came into my life. We met online and although we were both "geographically undesirable," I drove out to Phoenix to meet her and the rest, as they say, is history; we have been married now for almost a decade.

I owe my real first connection to Jewish music to Karen who introduced me to Craig Taubman, a well-known Jewish musician. He asked me about what I did and I shared my music with him. I ended up performing with Craig several times over the next couple of years, and he was the one who introduced me to Dr. Bruce Powell and the New Community Jewish High School.

NCJHS, or New Jew, as it is called, was a fairly new Jewish high school, but it was expanding rapidly. When I took the position as instrumental band director, they were entering their third year of existence. I had no idea what to expect. With very little of my own Jewish knowledge, I just assumed that the kids who went to a Jewish high school would be interested in Jewish music. I thought of Klezmer music and some of the classic Jewish songs I had heard growing up. I put together a curriculum that incorporated some of that type of music and also made some connections between Jewish music and other cultures - like Rastafarian culture and Reggae that incorporated Jewish melodies but modernized the settings and instrumentation. When I actually arrived in the classroom, I was surprised to find that the students were not necessarily all that connected to their own Jewish heritage. They wanted to play Green Day, blink-182, Fall Out Boy and Muse. I felt old, out of touch, and unprepared.

Then, Dr. Powell explained my role at the school to me. He said, "We can capture our students' minds and intellect with biology, literature and mathematics. Your job is to capture their hearts with the music." He envisioned a classroom in which the Tanakh was open and whether or not we were actually reading from the book, that somehow our efforts would be informed (through spiritual osmosis) by the Jewish wisdom contained in the books.

I was skeptical at first and did not know how that approach would translate to the students. I knew that the kids were not open to the more traditional Jewish music, so as a songwriter, I began working with them to create our own body of work that was loosely connected to our shared Judaism.

We started with the basics. If there was a holiday coming up we would talk about the major themes, how we could apply them to our own lives and how we could represent them musically. Sometimes, it would work in reverse. We would come up with a cool musical idea and then try to figure out how to connect it to some Jewish concept. We would write a song in 6/4 time signature and then discuss: where do we find the number six in Judaism? Well, there are six days and then Shabbat. And in the creation story, God creates man and woman on the sixth day and then takes a break. So, how does that apply to us? There was always an emphasis on making the concept real and accessible to the students, so the knowledge and wisdom did not exist outside of their everyday reality, but rather was incorporated and integrated into their lives. So, after our discussion, we would come to broader realizations like comparing the six days to relationships where there are different stages. You meet the person ("first day"); then the relationship develops over time ("second through fifth days") and finally on the "sixth day" you come together in an embrace or a shared connection. We created lyrics and music that reflected the students' understanding of these complex concepts in a way that could be understood and appreciated on a multitude of different levels.

The typical pop song has one or two different levels of depth. It's a love song. It's a happy song. It's a breakup song. These are the types of easily digestible compositions that are in demand in mainstream music. I found that the types of assignments that I was giving my students were actually very intriguing to me as well. I began giving myself the same kinds of assignments. I would take a quote or a piece of text and try to figure out how I could apply it to my own life. One of my first compositions of this type was called "Tree of Life." In doing my research, I found that the original Tree of Life in the Garden of Eden was surrounded by five hundred miles of another tree: the Tree of Knowledge. It was only by acquiring knowledge and experience that one was granted access to the Tree of Life. I incorporated much of this symbolism into my lyrics:

> *When the phone rang that day*
> *There was a voice from far away*
> *It was a wake-up call from home*
> *So I drove 500 miles for a hug and one last smile*
> *And I cried as he let go*

I used the idea of "passing wisdom from generation to generation" and made it real in my song:

Now the years flow by like water
As I look upon my daughter
I can see my grandpa's image looking back at me
I can almost hear his laughter
Coming through from Ever After
As I teach her of her family's famous legacy.

Suddenly, concepts that had previously existed only as abstract words on a page now had a human face and an emotional connection. It began to make sense to me and I started to value the wisdom that had always been a part of me but somehow had never made it to the surface. I had always wanted to "make a difference" with my music, but I didn't really know what that looked like. As I began to embrace my identity as a Jewish songwriter, I experienced first-hand how the music I was writing could impact whole communities and bring them together through song.

I can honestly say that if it were not for the music, I don't believe that my sense of my own Jewish identity would exist. I have always had a hard time accepting ideology because "this is the way we've always done things." Jewish music allows me to approach religion with fresh eyes because music is able to bypass the intellect. Even those who do not relate to traditional religion can still be moved to participate.

Throughout the years, I have seen and heard from many about the tangible difference that music has made in their lives – how it has

"I envision a kind of holistic Judaism where Jewish music and culture are as much a part of us as the air we breathe."

brought them together in community or helped them heal from a painful experience. The power of music in the world is palpable.

But the most profound impact that I observe from Jewish music is the effect that it has had on me. As much as I have resisted labeling myself as a "Jewish musician," I recognize that it is the music that has made me feel part of the Jewish community and that has given me a sense of my own identity as a Jewish man. I feel that my actions are now defined at least in part by principles that are expressed in Jewish texts and I feel a responsibility toward the Jewish community as a whole. I feel connected to something larger than myself.

Music is the vehicle through which I express myself, in which I invest my soul and the thing that transports me to a place that feels like home. My goal for my own music is to create a body of Jewish music that exists both within and outside of the synagogue. That is part of the reason I created the Desert Gathering Jewish Music Fest with the help of Valley Beit Midrash and Start Me Up! AZ (www.desertgatheringaz.com); we had our first show in November 2013. I want to give Jews in America and beyond the opportunity to experience their heritage and to feel proud about who they are no matter where they come from.

I envision a kind of holistic Judaism where Jewish music and culture are as much a part of us as the air we breathe. I imagine a world where we as Jews are proud of our identity, rather than the feelings of fragmented identity that is all too common for some American Jews today. And, I hope for a world where we can express our Judaism in our prayer and in our music and bring out the best in ourselves to our broader communities.

Todd Herzog is an artist who takes the material of life experiences and creates soulful, spiritual acoustic pop music that's at the intersection of John Mayer, Jason Mraz and Josh Groban. His mission is to use music to achieve a deeper understanding of life and spirituality and to share that understanding with others. He has worked with some of the top songwriters in the world, including Burt Bacharach, Dave Koz, Craig Taubman and Harriet Schock.

His award-winning music been featured in television and film in shows such as *Brotherhood*, *The Young and The Restless*, *All My Children*, *One Life To Live*, *Who Wants To Marry My Dad*, *The Osbournes*, and *Melrose Place*. Todd lives in Phoenix with his wife, Karen, and son, Sander. He performs at venues around the country and around the world, captivating and inspiring audiences of all ages.

The Power of
Jewish Summer Camp

Rabbi Stephen I. Kahn
Congregation Beth Israel

One of the great narratives in the Book of Numbers is the story found in Parshat Balak: With reports concerning the Israelites' defeat of the Amorites in the Kingdom of Sihon to the north of Moab, King Balak becomes fearful as the Israelites approach his border. He seeks the assistance of Balaam, a magician and soothsayer, to curse the Israelite. Balak commands Balaam to "put a curse upon this people for me, since they are too numerous for me."[1] As the story unfolds, we learn that on the way to fulfill his mission, Balaam has an epiphany and instead of cursing the Israelites he incants words of blessing. At the outset of his newfound words of praise, Balaam exclaims:

> How can I damn whom God has not damned.
> How doom when Adonai has not doomed?
> As I see them from the mountain tops,
> Gaze on them from the heights,
> There is a people that dwells alone[2]

Several commentaries explain that the phrase "dwells alone," was a blessing in that Balaam meant to praise Israel's elevated and regal status. However, the rabbis of the Talmud argue that Balaam's use of the Hebrew word l'vadav, "alone" was meant as a curse of the Israelites' status as a people who would never truly "fit in."

---

[1] JPS: The New JPS Translation According to the Traditional Hebrew Text (New York: Jewish Publication Society, 1988) Numbers 22:6
[2] Ibid. Numbers 23: 8-9

Former Chief Rabbi Lord Jonathan Sacks explains the Talmud's understanding of Balaam's comment "there is a people that dwells alone," in the following way: [that] Jews have long been cast in the role of the "other," the one who does not fit into the dominant paradigm, the majority faith, or the prevailing culture.[3]

Balaam's description of "a people that dwells alone," rings true today as well. Judaism can feel countercultural in contrast to the American condition - modernity makes it virtually impossible for many Jews to define being "alone" as anything other than a curse. In fact, maintaining a balanced Jewish life in the context of the infinite choices we have to "opt out" of Judaism altogether presents yet another curse as we strive to find ways, places and means with which to connect with other Jews in authentic ways. The most recent sociological and demographic studies that measure levels of identity, affiliation and Jewish commitment for North American Jews indicate that the ambivalent Jew is one who feels "alone," and distant from the heritage and traditions of our ancestors. Could it be that the strong influences of American pluralism and democracy have sociologically and psychologically driven Jews away from expressions of their Jewishness? Is living in separate communities where Jewish life is both necessary and sufficient to our happiness contrary to American values? What are the determining factors for the minority of American Jews who feel engaged in our communities, positively identified as part of the Jewish covenant and deeply connected to our Jewish world?

Like many American Jews of my generation, I am the product of Jewish parents and grandparents who were committed, affiliated and community-minded Jews. I am the beneficiary of a pluralistic Jewish upbringing. I attended Orthodox day school, became a Bar Mitzvah in a Conservative synagogue and was Confirmed in a Reform shul. My first experience at Jewish summer camp was at the age of 8 when I attended Chabad-Lubavich's Camp Gan Elohim in Berkeley, California.

While I was raised with an unambiguously Jewish identity as a child and a diverse religious background within my own

---

[3] Rabbi Jonathan Sacks, *Covenant and Conversation*, Balak (5771) "A People that Dwells Alone?" June 9, 2011.

community, I have always attributed the summer of 1988, when I became a staff member at the UAHC Camp Swig in Saratoga, California as the seminal experience in my Jewish life. It was at Jewish summer camp that I became acutely aware of what it meant to see the world through Jewish eyes and feel the blessings of "dwelling alone," in ways that would shape my future forever.

At Jewish summer camp I experienced for the first time in my life what it meant to be a member of an authentic Jewish community, a community that "dwells alone," in the best of all possible ways. Camp Swig was not just camp, it was comprised of a *Kehilah Kedosha* a "Holy Community," where God's presence was felt at all times, where Torah was not only learned but experienced and where Israel came to life through song and dance and engaging with our Israeli staff.

One of the great blessings of my life now is being given the opportunity of serving Congregation Beth Israel (CBI) in Scottsdale, Arizona, where I get to engage in the creation and development of the next generation of Jewish camping with our own Camp Daisy and Harry Stein in Prescott, Arizona. From both my experiences on staff at Camp Swig and now as the Rabbi of CBI, I am able to share my passion for Jewish camping with the next generation of campers and staff members in deeply rewarding ways.

These experiences at Jewish summer camp, for our staff and campers are the defining feature of their Jewish lives. For each of them, they "dwell alone" for eleven months of the year yearn for the opportunity to "dwelling alone" that feels more like a curse than a blessing. For many of our campers who come from communities with few, if any, Jewish families or are the products of Jewish-ly ambivalent parents and grandparents, they can feel a sense of deep loneliness without their Jewish camp community. Many come from communities where they do not feel positively unique but negatively different from others in their non-Jewish surroundings. In their home communities, even when their parents do affiliate with congregations, many still feel they are separate and apart from not a part of their communities. For our college-age staff members, their experiences on university campuses can often feel lonely as well. Jewish summer camp enables these students the experience of a safe and warm Jewish community built upon love and inclusion. Camp provides a sacred space where "dwelling alone" simply means the peace from college campuses, many of which are hostile toward Zionism, Israel and intolerant of diverse religious faith systems.

For our campers and staff, a summer at Jewish camp makes them feel safe, comfortable and "part of" not "apart from" their Jewish essence. Camp provides an environment in which "dwelling alone" is a blessing; a celebration of space and time Jewishly in a place that is uniquely Jewish. Jewish summer camp takes place exclusively on holy ground where the arts, recreation, sports, learning, praying, celebrating Shabbat, singing and dancing are all profound experiences because they cannot be replicated anywhere else. "Camp time," enables us to create a sense for our campers and staff where, within our implicit curriculum, we teach that it is not only acceptable to be uniquely Jewish, that being Jewish is a blessing to the world around us. Our campers and staff learn, whether they are conscious of it or not, that being part of the Jewish covenant means that we can make the world better and they experience a community where "dwelling alone" never means that we are actually alone.

At a leadership seminar for the Foundation for Jewish Camp, Chancellor Arnold Eisen, Ph.D, of the Jewish Theological Seminary eloquently described this ideal Jewish community dynamic[4] that can only be produced at a Jewish summer camp as follows:

> We Jews are here to build Jewish communities. We weren't chartered as a religious group alone; we were made a people. This means a set of global and local communities because communities can do things that individuals cannot. Communities can persuade people of the right and the true, even against the flow of a society in which others don't think that. Communities can help gather strength, can elicit the finest efforts and teach people to reach higher. When you teach lessons that you want to be real life lessons that you want to take hold of a person, especially when those lessons go against the grain of a society, against the taken-for-granted assumptions of the larger culture the teaching must be operative 24/7...

---

[4] Rabbi Arnold Eisen, "Seminary Leaders Panel," Foundation for Jewish Camp Leaders Assembly, March 22, 2012. https://www.youtube.com/watch?v=2LlcXWl8jSo

That's where camping in North America rises to the occasion of dealing with the reality...that for the most part does not place Jews, Jewish adults or Jewish kids, inside Jewish gates or Jewish doorposts for the majority of their lives. The Jewish part of life is usually off to the side, marginal to the main business of life. And so you need to create a counter reality such as a 24/7 Jewish camp.

The truth is, the 24/7 model of living in a holistic Jewish world in the ways of our ancestors - a world where every aspect of our Jewish lives supports and reinforces our Jewish identities – has been dismantled by our own secularization and success as Americans. This is not to say that we are not fully capable of creating models for Jewish learning, Jewish life, ritual and community that address the breakdown of Jewish life in modernity. Being anchored in a Jewish community, affiliated and participatory in the life of the synagogue, formal and informal Jewish education, Jewish day school and Jewish ritual are all important pieces to creating a system that supports our efforts to have Jewish grandchildren.

"We create a sense for our campers and staff where, within our implicit curriculum, we teach that it is not only acceptable to be uniquely Jewish, that being Jewish is a blessing to the world around us."

Yet, without the experience of Jewish summer camp as the fixed point of these experiences, our children and teens may never pragmatically know what an organic "24/7" Jewish community looks like and feels like. This experience is, singularly, the most potent antidote to the Jewish loneliness our kids feel outside of this sacred space and time.

Rabbi Stephen I. Kahn is the Senior Rabbi of Congregation Beth Israel in Scottsdale, Arizona. Rabbi Kahn was born and raised in San Francisco, California. After receiving his Bachelor's degree from the University of California, Santa Cruz in Politics, he attended the Hebrew Union College-Jewish Institute of Religion in Jerusalem, Los Angeles and New York where he received rabbinic ordination in 1995.

Prior to his arrival at Congregation Beth Israel in 2003, Rabbi Kahn served as Assistant Rabbi at Temple Sinai in Denver, Colorado and Associate Rabbi-Educator at Congregation Sherith Israel in San Francisco. He currently serves on the President's Rabbinic Cabinet of HUC-JIR. Rabbi Kahn has been married to Michele L. Kahn, LCSW, for almost two decades and together they have three children: Ethan, Gabrielle and Isabel.

The Power of the Particular to Realize the Universal

Rabbi John A. Linder
Senior Rabbi
Temple Solel

As a child, growing up in a secular Jewish home in Buffalo, New York, I was drawn to the American vision of the melting pot. I loved the metaphor that we are all in the same boat – people pulling on the oars together for the common good. I thought that differentiating one another religiously, racially, culturally or nationally was divisive. I associated these differences with fanning the flames of bigotry, discrimination and xenophobia. Religion, in particular, rubbed me the wrong way. I saw religion as pitting one truth against another's truth. I saw religion as the enemy of reason. I saw religion as license for the murder of hundreds of thousands, of different faiths or no faiths, all in the name of God.

At the same time, I viewed my liberal arts education as a way to reinforce the universal ideal of our common humanity. It was my college roommate, Paul Vogel, who thought it would be a great experience to travel to Israel one summer and work on a kibbutz together. Indeed, it was an amazing summer. I fell in love with Israel. One Friday morning, we traveled from Kibbutz Gvat, located in northern Israel's Jezreel Valley, to Jerusalem. Like many young, impressionable American Jews, we surely stood out in our eagerness, walking into the Old City through the Jaffa Gate. No sooner had we bought fresh sesame rolls from the push cart of a young Arab man, than a young, clearly Jewish man, with a black hat, *peyos*, *tzitzit* hanging from his waist, approached us with a fervent stride. After confirming our Jewish identity, asking only if our mothers were Jews, he invited us to a

Shabbos dinner at "the rebbe's" house. Paul and I surely hadn't thought through our dinner plans by that point, and a free, hot meal sounded like a great offer. We gratefully accepted.

The evening at the rebbe's house felt like an anthropological field trip. It may have been the first Shabbos dinner, complete with rituals that I had ever experienced. Quite honestly, I felt more at home at my friend, Nelson Tanner Montgomery III's, house on a Friday evening than at the rebbe's house. After a festive meal, joyful singing and more than our share of schnapps (who knew this was a Shabbos requirement?) the rebbe directly invited Paul and me to come visit his yeshiva in the Old City of Jerusalem on Sunday morning. Paul and I, with some combination of inebriation and recognition that this was the price of the meal, respectfully accepted the invitation.

"Our mission, in partnership with God, is to continue the work of creation - to join hands with peoples of all faiths as messengers of peace and justice."

The field trip continued. One of the rebbe's students gave us a tour of the yeshiva. I was astounded to meet a Jew from Dublin, intently bent over some timeworn, leather-bound Hebrew text that looked like it was brought down from Mt. Sinai. Growing up, with lots of Irish friends from South Buffalo, I for sure had never met an Irish Jew. Paul and I sat in on the rebbe's class, taught in English, to young Jews like us from America, Canada, South Africa, Australia, England and yes, Ireland. I must say that I was engrossed in whatever it was the rebbe was teaching. He touched a chord. An aware teacher is tuned in to those students with whom he or she has connected. The rebbe knew he had me.

When the lesson was done, I came to the front of the class and thanked the rebbe, shaking his hand. My friend Paul was by my side. While shaking hands, the rebbe looked me straight in the eyes and asked, "Do you believe that God gave Moses the Ten Commandments on Mt. Sinai?" I did not understand what he was really asking, but indicated so with a tentative, affirmative nod of the head. The rebbe then tried to close the deal. He went on to invite me to stay and study at his yeshiva, instead of returning to my *goyishe*, liberal arts, cloistered, New England college (for his cloistered, fundamentalist yeshiva in Old Jerusalem). At this point, Paul was a little concerned he'd be returning to the States without his friend John. While the rebbe had indeed tapped a chord deep inside, there was just something about the certainty of his beliefs that raised a red flag. In the face of this powerful man who had the key to God and authentic Judaism, I gave some pathetic, unformed excuse why I could not make such a commitment. Paul was relieved. I followed him out of the yeshiva like a puppy with my tail between my legs.

After graduating from college, my sense of kindred spirits with peoples of all faiths and ethnicities, and commitment to social justice, led me to serve as a community and labor organizer. As a community organizer with Massachusetts Fair Share, I worked in Boston's working class neighborhood of Roslindale. I so clearly remember Orca, a Greek Orthodox woman, Yves, a Christian Lebanese man, Roland, of Scottish descent, and Gladys, a Jewish woman from Eastern Europe. I felt so alive and engaged in meaningful work – bringing together this diverse group of people, joined by their common interests in making their neighborhood, city, state and country a better place. I loved it, though I felt there was something missing.

As a labor organizer in Columbus, Ohio, for the Hospital and Health Care Workers Union, 1199, AFL-CIO, I so clearly remember Gary and Collette, a bi-racial husband and wife working as hospital aids; Sherry, a white RN; Renee, a black LPN in her 40s with three grandchildren; Evelyn, a white food service worker from Appalachia, and Anish, a psychiatrist from India. What brought this incredibly diverse group of people together was a common commitment to fairness, justice, and quality patient care. Union organizing exists in a tension-filled, highly charged environment. I spent one afternoon in a jail cell, handcuffs, mug shot and all, because I was a "threat" to the hospital superintendent. It was an all-out, purpose-driven experience like I'd never had. I loved it, though I knew there was something missing; just couldn't quite put my finger on it.

I met my beloved Nancy Levy during those years in Columbus. (Thankfully, she said yes to be my bride). Yet, round-the-clock shifts at the hospitals, meeting workers in the parking lot, in their break rooms, in the florescent glow of White Castle, didn't bode well for us as newlyweds. I spent little time with my wife. My fellow organizers were deeply dedicated to the cause of workers' rights; and they were workaholics, hard drinkers who left a trail of broken relationships and marriages. That scared me. I didn't want my marriage to be collateral damage to organizing and my passion for social justice. I left organizing and Nancy and I moved back to my hometown of Buffalo, where I went to work in the family scrap metal recycling business. Nancy and I were blessed with a son, David, indeed our beloved one. We wanted to ground him more deeply in Judaism than either of us was grounded. Acting on that desire transformed us as a Jewish family.

We enrolled David in the preschool at Temple Beth Am, and I began learning the *alef-bet* along with our son. I attended Torah study for the first time, led by Rabbi Steven Mason. I was immediately struck by the confluence of the universal and the particular in Judaism. Our story begins with the creation of humanity; each of us created in the image of God – then

"Being a Jew is to be a lover of humanity and all of God's creation – the intersection of the particular and the universal."

flows into the birth of the Jewish people, beginning with Abraham and Sarah. God anticipates our question, why was Abraham chosen to be the patriarch of the Jewish people, and provides an answer: "because he will do what is right and just."[1] Our mission, in partnership with God, is to continue the work of creation – to join hands with peoples of all faiths as messengers of peace and justice.

This was an "a-ha" moment for me – the missing piece that I could not put my finger on as a community and labor organizer was Judaism. Little did I know that my own Jewish faith obligates us to pursue justice and seek peace. Yet, in contrast to the rebbe in Jerusalem many years earlier, this was a Judaism that embraced reason and allowed for multiple truths; a Judaism that embraced the

---

[1] Genesis 18:19

story and lessons of Sinai, not the historicity of Sinai. I was no longer (to paraphrase George Santayana) spinning my wheels to speak in general without any language in particular. I now had a language, thousands of years of divinely inspired words that gave me a voice to speak and a lens through which to see the world.

The more immersed in Judaism, the more connected to Israel and the Jewish people I became, the more comfortable I felt in my own skin, as a member of the human family. Judaism stretched my mind, opened my heart and nourished my soul. Our tradition, at its core, is about how we treat one another and care for the earth entrusted to us. Though Judaism does not have the market cornered on ethics, morally driven choices are our currency that continues to flow down the slopes of Sinai. Our sacred texts and rituals exist to inspire, remind us of our obligations and stir us to action.

The Jewish particular is with us when we lie down and when we rise up – in private and communal prayer, in touching a mezuzah on the doorposts of our house and place of work, in gratitude before and after a meal, in praising God throughout the day for the miracles that surrounds us, in consecrating the holiness of Shabbat, in keeping the sweetness of Shabbat with us throughout the week, in traveling to Israel, observing the yearly holiday cycle, giving *tzedakah*, honoring our parents, visiting the sick, celebrating with the bride and groom, accompanying the dead for burial, being messengers of peace, *v'talmud Torah, k'neged kulam* – and the study of Torah is our greatest obligation, because it leads to acts of goodness in the world.[2]

Yet, if the particular becomes an end unto itself and eclipses the universal, our tradition keeps us in check. The prophet Isaiah paints an interfaith, multi-cultural vision of what the world will look like when humanity is one and at peace: the messianic age. "In that day there will be an altar to the Lord in the heart of Egypt, and a monument to the Lord at its border. It will be a sign and witness to the Lord Almighty in the Land of Egypt. When they cry out to the Lord because of their oppressors, He will send them a savior and defender, and He will rescue them..."In that day there will be a highway from Egypt to Assyria... In that day Israel will be the third, along with Egypt and Assyria, a blessing on earth. The Lord Almighty will bless them, saying, 'Blessed be Egypt my people,

[2] Adapted from the morning blessings, *V'ahavtah* and *Eilu D'varim*

Assyria my handiwork, and Israel my inheritance.'"[3]

Emanuel Levinas, drawing on Talmudic legend, reminded us that, "In the cave that represents the resting place of our patriarchs and matriarchs, also lays Adam and Eve to rest; it is for the whole of humanity that Judaism came into the world."[4] Our place as Jews lies at intersection of the particular and the universal.

3 Isaiah 19:19-25

4 Emmanuel Levinas, *Difficult Freedom: Essays on Judaism*, translated by Sean Hand (Baltimore: John's Hopkins University Press, 1990), essay on Israel and Universalism, 176.

Rabbi John A. Linder was born in Buffalo NY – always proud of his hometown. After graduating cum laude as an American Studies major at Amherst College, Rabbi Linder spent six years as a community and labor organizer for Massachusetts Fair Share and the Hospital and Health Care Workers Union, 1199, AFL-CIO.

At the age of 41, Rabbi Linder entered his first year of rabbinic school at Hebrew Union College – Jewish institute of Religion. He received his Master's in Hebrew Letters in 2002 and was ordained in 2003. He served as an Assistant/Associate Rabbi at B'nai Jehoshua Beth Elohim in Chicago, before moving to Arizona in 2008 to serve as Senior Rabbi of Temple Solel in Paradise Valley. Nationally, John is a leader in the Union for Reform Judaism's social justice work through Just Congregations and the Religious Action Center, and serves on the Board of the Chicago Theological Seminary. Locally, Rabbi Linder is actively involved in the Phoenix Board of Rabbis, Jewish Family and Children's Services, Anti-Defamation League, Human Rights Campaign, Association of the United States Army, Arizona Career Pathways and Valley Interfaith Project.

In the summer of 2013, John competed in the Maccabiah Games in Israel, winning the gold medal as a member of the USA Masters Ice Hockey Team. Rabbi Linder counts his blessings for the love of his family and friends, and the daily gift to sanctify God's name by bringing alive the words of our sacred texts in our everyday lives.

The Power of Traditional Jewish Observance

Rabbi Reuven Mann
Young Israel of Phoenix

The observance of Purim is, arguably, the most joyous occasion on the Jewish calendar. There is no prohibition against performing ordinary weekday activities and its most challenging religious requirement is to listen to the reading of the Megillah, the Book of Esther written on a scroll. Otherwise, it's a happy day with a festive meal, distribution of treats to one's friends and gifts to the poor. A sense of unity prevails among the Jews as we celebrate the salvation of our people from the edict of annihilation instigated by the evil Haman.

The theme of deliverance from our enemies is central to the Jewish historical experience. We are a people who live in the shadow of hatred and are always on the verge of a major catastrophe. At the Passover *seder*, we recite: "In every generation they rise against us to destroy us, but the Holy One, blessed is He, saves us from their hands."

However, for American Jews, the history of anti-Semitism and religious oppression is abstract and remote from personal experience. As a kid in the 1950s, I did encounter some verbal bigotry and bullying from non-Jewish kids. That was the time when expressions of prejudice were still "acceptable." Thankfully, matters have changed dramatically during the course of my life. In the last fifty years or so, the country has thankfully undergone a major transformation on the issue of tolerance. It now categorically condemns all forms of bigotry based on race, religion, color, gender, and sexual orientation.

We have witnessed the election of an African-American president, which was inconceivable when I was growing up. It was once regarded as a self-evident truth that there could never be a Jewish president. In 2000, on the Gore-Lieberman ticket,

Joseph Lieberman's "Jewishness" was not viewed as a drawback; in fact, many voters regarded it in a positive light.

We must acknowledge that never in our history have we, as Jews, attained such freedom and acceptance. Every area of endeavor is open to us, and Jews no longer have to change their names in order to succeed.

As a youngster, I felt awkward and uncomfortable getting up to pray in a public place such as an airport. Today, I have no compunctions at all putting on *tallit* and *tefillin* in an airport terminal. I even pray on airplanes when necessary and receive nothing but respectful understanding from my fellow passengers. In fact, one time, a Catholic woman asked me to say a prayer for her sister who was ill with cancer. As a Jewish comedian who hailed from Russia once said, "America, what a country!"

From the standpoint of freedom, respect and acceptance, the United States has been a great home for us. However, when I think of our sojourn here, Charles Dickens's famous line applies: "It was the best of times, it was the worst of times." We can no longer ignore the awesome spiritual price we have paid for our time in America. Sadly, Jews have become one of the least religious groups in this country. The rates of assimilation and intermarriage threaten the continuity of the Jewish community. All sectors of the Jewish community have been shocked most by the Pew demographic study released in 2013. It documents a 70 percent intermarriage rate and a frightening dissolution of the concept of Jewish identity. American Jews are renouncing Judaism or watering down its essence to what I fear is the point of meaninglessness. If these trends continue, we are in serious trouble. In fact, I propose that we officially designate American Jews as an endangered species.

We must also consider this perplexing dilemma: Our history in the exile has been a constant struggle to obtain full political rights and acceptance; yet it has been the times of struggle and rejection that have brought us together as a people. As long as the Jew was mistreated, segregated, or severely limited in his economic opportunities, he was steadfast in his adherence to his faith. We must ask, is Judaism sustainable only in conditions of persecution? Can it survive the era of American freedom and acceptance? Can it compete with the material allurements and moral relativism of this society? What lessons must we learn from the Pew

Report?

There is one positive statistic in this otherwise dreary survey: assimilation and intermarriage numbers drop precipitously among the various groups that identify as Orthodox. The report shows that Jews who are strictly observant and teach their religion to their children by placing them in religious day schools seem to be the most successful in perpetuating Jewish identity in contemporary America.

America has gone through a cultural and sexual revolution that has deemphasized the family and religious values in favor of a materialistic and hedonistic philosophy that glorifies "doing your own thing" at the expense of long-held moral and societal guidelines. These attitudes are diametrically opposed to the fundamental principles of Judaism. I am sorry to say that anyone whose views are shaped by the current culture will not take our Torah-based religion very seriously.

"From the standpoint of freedom, respect and acceptance, the United States has been a great home for us...However, we can no longer ignore the awesome spiritual price we have paid for our time in America."

American Jewish leaders must not stand idly by as this crisis unfolds. We must not repeat our failure to aggressively advocate for vigorous rescue policies during the Holocaust, when Jews were threatened with physical annihilation. The spiritual form of religious decimation that faces us today could also lead to Jewish annihilation. Can we adopt a posture of indifference and continue business as usual? Or, like Mordechai in the Megillah, should we not don sackcloth and ashes and go into the streets and "scream a loud and bitter scream?" If we don't feel this sense of responsibility to our fellow Jews, we will be of no real help to them.

The current crisis is a test of the depth of our commitment to Judaism and the future of our people. Everyone should ask himself, "Do I truly believe in the veracity of Torah and the teachings of Judaism, or do the basic tenets of American culture take prominence?"

When I read the Pew Report, it seemed to demonstrate that only Judaism based on absolute commitment to the divinity of Torah and observance of the commandments, as they have been transmitted through the ages, is sustainable. The Jewish religion has survived the most turbulent circumstances because, throughout our history, the Jews have regarded themselves as God's Chosen People, whose mission was to scrupulously observe the commandments. If we deny our mission as a people, the divine origin of our Torah, and our absolute obligation to perform the *mitzvot*, we are threatening our own existence as a people and making the current crisis worse for ourselves.

In my opinion, it is vital that we appreciate the uniqueness of Judaism and stand together as a people. Our conviction in the divine character of Torah motivates us to devote our energy to its study. When we immerse ourselves in Torah learning, we become aware of its limitless depth and incomparable beauty. The social calamities that plague our country, such as the breakdown of the family, the monumental increase in drug abuse and dependencies, excessive violence, and the inability to sustain meaningful relationships, are but some of the symptoms of a culture that rejects God and His Laws.

We must reorient ourselves to the Torah. We must study it with energy and passion, and mold our behavior according to its principles. Then, we will fulfill our mission as God's people and be a source of blessing to ourselves and our children and a light unto the nations.

Rabbi Reuven Mann is the spiritual leader of Young Israel of Phoenix. In addition to his decades as a dynamic pulpit rabbi, and sought-after speaker, he has a distinguished career in Jewish education.

As a founder and *menahel* (principal) of the post-high school Yeshiva B'nei Torah in Far Rockaway, New York, Rabbi Mann has trained many leading American rabbis and educators. He is also the founder and dean of the Masoret Institute of Advanced Judaic Studies for Women in Inwood, New York.

The Power of Interfaith Relations

Rabbi Jeremy Schneider
Temple Kol Ami

I am Jewish and I believe in the power of Interfaith Relations. In fact, having been born and raised in Houston, Texas, it's probably fair to say that I was born into interfaith relations. While Judaism is not the first thing that comes to mind when thinking about Texas, there is actually a large collection of Jewish Texans. I grew up learning to say "Yes, Ma'am," and "No, Sir," believing I actually was living in the "Promised Land." Our worship service occasionally ended with "Ya'll come back now, ya hear?"

Growing up, my parents taught me that Judaism was my primary spiritual language. This language includes reciting the *Shema*, celebrating new life with a naming ceremony in the synagogue or home, marking our coming of age with a Bar/Bat Mitzvah ceremony, binding ourselves to a love partner under the *chuppah* with the blessings of wine, and facing the death of loved ones with specific mourning customs. Thanks to my parents, Judaism also became the central language to observe sacred time: Shabbat, Rosh Hashanah, Yom Kippur, Sukkot, Chanukah and Passover.

I never thought to ask whether my religion was better than others, just as I would never ask whether English is better than other languages. Or if Hebrew is better than Latin. I became fluent in my language of Judaism, which gave me a rich, strong and clear identity.

Judaism is – in many ways – my life story. My Jewish beliefs structure and nurture how I experience this world. It influences how I pray and celebrate; how I cope with life's darker side, and how I understand that there is meaning beyond the mystery. I have come to appreciate the nuances of Judaism – particularly how Jews are sustained through the power of a close-knit community. And I have been encased in the centrality of the mitzvah, my Jewish responsibilities. These beliefs allow me to bear witness to God and, at the same time, struggle with God.

Growing up in Texas among a primarily non-Jewish community thickened my skin. It strengthened my resolve, and turned me not just into a practicing Jew, but a teacher of Judaism. And – as Jews – our wisdom increases as we learn from others. Who is wise? Our tradition teaches us that the answer is "One who learns from ALL people" (*Ethics of the Fathers*, 4:1). I find that the more I interact with others who have a rich, strong and clear identity, the more I learn about myself, my faith and my role as a Jewish professional and spiritual leader.

"I believe in the truths of many other worldviews. Wisdom is the ability to learn from all humans and points of view. Such open-mindedness can only strengthen our religion, faith, and resolve."

From Christians I knew growing up and those with whom I currently work, I have learned about faith. If Jews speak of a leap of action, Christians speak of a leap of faith. It gives Christians serenity and an acceptance of adversity, which I admire. As a Jew, I am always ready to argue with God. But maybe there comes a time to simply say that I believe in God and I trust in God.

From Muslims I work with, I have learned about surrender. After all, the very name Islam means submitting to God. Judaism tends to emphasize the power of humans as God's partners; Islam focuses on human limitations in the face of God's presence. Again, there is a time for arguing with God and a time to surrender to a force greater than ourselves.

I have also learned from the religions of the Far East - Buddhism and Hinduism. If Judaism emphasizes how to live in this world, the religions of the East accept this world as a place of suffering and, ultimately, non-reality. They have developed pathways to a spiritual connection with the world, whether through meditation, yoga, or other spiritual practices. They have developed an entire science of the inner self and inner mind that has become influential in the West, including Kabbalah. The East has powerful insights to teach Judaism and me.

I have even learned from atheism, which is best summed up

by a well-known story told in Jewish circles: A rabbi tells his students that they can learn valuable lessons from everything God put on the earth. One student challenges the rabbi. "What can we learn from atheism?" The rabbi replies, "We can learn a great deal from atheism. When you see your brother or sister in trouble, do not say `God will take care of you.' Act as if there is no God, and everything is in your hands."

I am Jewish and I believe in the power of Interfaith Relations. Indeed, I believe in the truths of many other worldviews. Wisdom is the ability to learn from all humans and points of view. Such open-mindedness can only strengthen our religion, faith, and resolve.

Rabbi Jeremy Schneider is the spiritual leader of Temple Kol Ami in Scottsdale and vice president of the Greater Phoenix Board of Rabbis. A native of Houston, Rabbi Schneider attended the University of Texas, Austin where he earned his Bachelor's degree in Applied Learning and Development. He attended and earned a Master's degree while at rabbinical school at the Hebrew Union College – Jewish Institute of Religion.

Rabbi Schneider has done extensive work in the field of interfaith relations: In 2014, he completed a yearlong Interfaith Fellowship Seminar with the Monsignor Ryle Fund and in 2012, he was selected to be a Brickner Fellow by the Religious Action Center in Washington, DC.

In 2009, Rabbi Schneider was selected to participate in the executive leadership program Synagogues: Transformation and Renewal: Professional Education for Excellence in the Rabbinate; The *Jewish News of Greater Phoenix*, Union for Reform Judaism and *Reflections and Experiences of Religion and Society*, have published his writings.

In 2008, Rabbi Schneider was chosen as one of six Americans for an interfaith study tour in Egypt and Syria sponsored by the U.S. Department of State. The following year he was given the "Citizen Diplomat – Peace Quilt Award" from the National Peace Foundation in Washington, D.C. for his grassroots works in durable peace building.

Rabbi Schneider is married to Rachel and is the proud father of Ezra, Micah, and Naomi.

The Power of Transformative Wisdom

Rabbi Dr. Shmuly Yanklowitz
Executive Director
Valley Beit Midrash

We are all yearning to understand something deeper, something beyond ourselves. Rabbi Shimshon Raphael Hirsch taught that the blessing of *hamalach ha'goel*, given to children, is that we should be like fish that can swim to depths that humans treading on the surface cannot see. There are many different types of wisdom that we can embrace. Rabbi Jonathan Sacks, for example, teaches that secular wisdom (*chokhmah*) is a philosophical orientation while the Torah is normative:

> *Chokhmah* is the truth we discover; Torah is the truth we inherit. *Chokhmah* is the universal language of humankind; Torah is the specific inheritance of the Israel. *Chokhmah* is what we attain by being in the image of God; Torah is what guides Jews as the people of God. *Chokhmah* is acquired by seeing and reasoning; Torah is received by listening and responding. *Chokhmah* tells us what is; Torah tell us what ought to be. (*Future Tense*, 221).

He adds that "*Chokhmah* is where we encounter God through creation; Torah is how we hear God through revelation" (The Chief Rabbi's Hagaddah, essays section, 6).

But intellectual synergy can be difficult because of how different our fundamental philosophical orientations can be. The French-born author Anaïs Nin writes: "We don't see things as they are, we see things as we are." Nin is touching on the larger point that for human beings there is no unfiltered reality.

"Judaism mandates that our learning be transformative and translate into character development and behavioral change."

All objective data must pass and be processed through the subjective mind to be experienced. This processing is what social psychologist Erich Fromm referred to as our "frame of orientation." While this may be a societal problem (understanding each other), it is also an individual opportunity. American dancer/choreographer Martha Graham wrote to Agnes DeMille, another American dancer/choreographer, about the importance of cultivating our unique wisdom and energy:

> There is a vitality, a life force, a quickening that is translated through you into action. And because there is only one of you in all time, this expression is unique. If you block it, it will never exist through any other medium and be lost. The world will not hear it. It is not your business to determine how good it is; nor how valuable it is; not how it compares with other expressions. It is your business to keep it yours, clearly and directly, to keep the channel open. You do not even need to believe in yourself or your work. You have to keep open and aware directly to the urges that motivate you. Keep the channel open. No artist is pleased. There is no satisfaction at any time. There is only a divine dissatisfaction, a blessed unrest that keeps us marching and makes us more alive than others.

Many hide from attaining wisdom for this reason – that it is challenging to understand others, sometimes even unpleasant. Many others refrain from transformative learning because of the new responsibilities that would emerge with such a new understanding. These concerns are well founded, because it is true that once we understand on an elevated plane of reality, we may become very powerful. Consider the wisdom of Nelson Mandela's words from his inaugural address:

> Our deepest fear is not that we are inadequate. Our deepest fear is that we are powerful beyond measure. It is our light not our darkness that frightens us. Actually, who are you not to be? You are a child of God. Your playing small doesn't serve the world. There's nothing enlightened about shrinking so that other people won't feel insecure around you. We were born to make manifest the glory of God that is within us.

When we come to understand our unique position and potential in the world, we can become terrified by how much needs to be done. To stay focused on learning and growing, we must have positive supports and a healthy lifestyle. The great Maimonides taught that two different types of wisdom could help to heal one from sadness and alienation

> If one is afflicted with melancholy, he should cure it by listening to songs and various kinds of the melodies, by walking in gardens and fine buildings, by sitting before beautiful forms, and by things like this which delight the soul and make the disturbance of melancholy disappear from it. In all this he should aim at making his body healthy, the goal of his body's health being that he attain knowledge (Introduction to his Commentary on *Pirkei Avot*, Chapter 5).

Secondly, Rambam suggested:

> What is a remedy for sicknesses of the soul? Go next to wise people, for they are healers of the soul, healing it by means of temperaments which they teach until they have returned the soul to the good ways. Concerning those who recognize in themselves bad temperaments but do not amongst wise people Solomon said, "Fools despise wisdom and instruction" (*Mishnah Torah, Deot* 2:1).

Maimonides taught that we should put ourselves in beautiful natural environments that elevate the soul sensually, and furthermore, surround ourselves with people of wisdom. We must position ourselves for a lifelong journey of learning. The National Endowment for the Arts recently released the shocking statistic that only 47 percent of Americans said they read a book for pleasure last year. This is not only shocking, but also profoundly unfortunate. Learning should not just be interesting, or helpful, or even just personally healing; learning can, and should, be much more. Judaism mandates that our learning be transformative and translate into character development and behavioral change.

Regardless of the newfound understanding of others, responsibilities, or ethical obligations that may accompany such transformative learning, we must not shun the philosophical and intellectual revelation that comes from deeper understanding of God and our world.

We must embrace our intellectual capabilities, mental faculties, and spiritual yearnings, and seek deeper wisdom. It is through consistent transformative learning that we develop our intellect, empathy, and dedication to service that subsequently leads us to fulfill our unique roles enhancing the world.

CLOSING WORDS

I am so grateful to our writers and editors for partnering to produce this wonderful journal. Together we are building an enhanced culture of Jewish intellectual life in Phoenix, and hopefully around the world. Jewish thought is at the center of our tradition and the Valley Beit Midrash is committed to finding as many different avenues for learning as possible (classes, speakers, panels, journals, and videos, etc.).

The Jewish people are remarkably multifaceted. Despite our differing perspectives on various issues, there is so much that ties us together. It is our belief that this diversity, when in dialogue, makes us richer. I hope that you'll take the time not only to read an article from a rabbi that you know and love, but also from one that you don't know and who you suspect holds very different commitments from your own.

In our complex era, it is more important than ever to reflect upon the topic of this issue's journal: "The Power of Being Jewish." Each of us must write our own story. While we may be inspired by another's journey, we must ultimately develop our own path that we own and love. Judaism is, inherently, very powerful. It is my prayer and hope that we as Jews can find our own unique power in the tradition and that it can enable us to find – and thrive – in our life purpose.

- Rabbi Dr. Shmuly Yanklowitz

15202969R00078

Made in the USA
San Bernardino, CA
18 September 2014